THE SECRET LOVES OF GEEKS

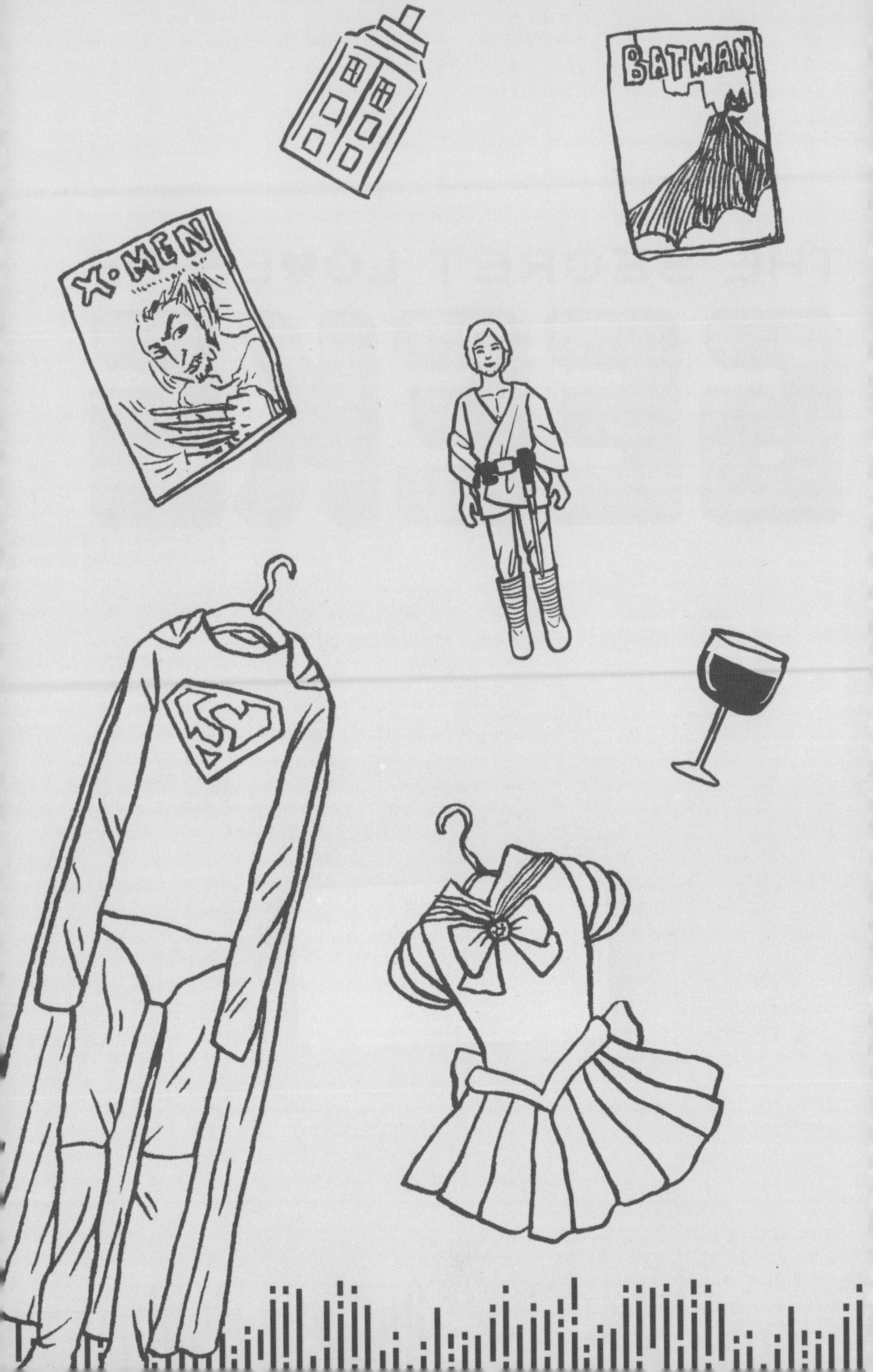
X-MEN
BATMAN

THE SECRET LOVES OF
GEEKS

EDITED BY HOPE NICHOLSON
COVER ART BY BECKY CLOONAN

DARK HORSE BOOKS

President and Publisher **MIKE RICHARDSON**
Collection Editors **DANIEL CHABON** and **CARDNER CLARK**
Designer **SARAH TERRY**
Digital Art Technician **CHRISTINA McKENZIE**

Neil Hankerson Executive Vice President | **Tom Weddle** Chief Financial Officer | **Randy Stradley** Vice President of Publishing | **Nick McWhorter** Chief Business Development Officer | **Matt Parkinson** Vice President of Marketing | **David Scroggy** Vice President of Product Development | **Dale LaFountain** Vice President of Information Technology | **Cara Niece** Vice President of Production and Scheduling | **Mark Bernardi** Vice President of Book Trade and Digital Sales | **Ken Lizzi** General Counsel | **Dave Marshall** Editor in Chief | **Davey Estrada** Editorial Director | **Scott Allie** Executive Senior Editor | **Chris Warner** Senior Books Editor | **Cary Grazzini** Director of Specialty Projects | **Lia Ribacchi** Art Director | **Vanessa Todd** Director of Print Purchasing | **Matt Dryer** Director of Digital Art and Prepress | **Michael Gombos** Director of International Publishing and Licensing

Published by Dark Horse Books
A division of Dark Horse Comics, Inc.
10956 SE Main Street | Milwaukie, OR 97222

First edition: February 2018
ISBN 978-1-50670-473-9

10 9 8 7 6 5 4 3 2 1
Printed in China

International Licensing: (503) 905-2377 | To find a comics shop in your area, visit comicshoplocator.com

THE SECRET LOVES OF GEEKS

TABLE OF CONTENTS

INTRODUCTION

By **HOPE NICHOLSON**

Welcome to *The Secret Loves of Geeks*!

Spoiler Warning: This introduction contains descriptions of the stories within! I recommend you read the book first, then circle back around to this intro afterwards.

This anthology is a collection of stories by comic book creators, video game critics, actors, and passionate fans of various fandoms. What they have in common is that they all share our true, painful, funny, and joyful experiences about the world of love, sex, and dating.

Now, that doesn't mean that every story is sexy! There's nothing less sexy than talking about how you pretended to love *Star Wars* for a year just to connect with your then-boyfriend (like in JP Larocque's "Love in Alderaan Places"). And not every story is *about* sex either—there are stories about asexuality like Shee Phon's "Do You Feel It," a soft portrait of the disconnect between romantic hugging and sexual smooching. Some of our stories are about the idols we worship, like Dylan Edward's "Ace Pilot," Sfé Monster's "Tell Me About Your Trans Headcanons," Ivan Salazar's "The Walter Mercado Effect," and Gwen Benaway's "Becoming the Slayer," each one a story about recognizing aspects of yourself, your sexuality, and your gender in the heroes you watch on screen.

Some stories are about the non-sexual loves of our lives—whether that's best friends, like in Letty Wilson's "Smudged" comic, or your children, in Patrick Rothfuss's "The Multifarious Monolith of Love."

Some stories are about past loves that stay in our hearts forever, like MariNaomi's "Star Struck," a comic about the annoyances of dating someone famous in certain circles, Levi Hasting's "So Say We All," about the pain of grief and loss, Cecil Castellucci's story about finding love while camped out for *The Phantom Menace*, and Vita Ayala's "Dear First Love," about all the lovers who've left positive marks—even if your time together was brief.

Others are about lovers currently with us: Dana Simpson's gently amusing story of finding her partner—and discovering herself—through furry fandom in "Deceptively Normal," Amanda Deibert and Cat Staggs building a family together in "Harry Potter and the Awkward Coming Out Story," the changing fluidity of your partner's gender in H-P Lehkonen's comic "Wife," and discovering a new passion together in Shauna J. Grant's comic "Our Story."

Many of the stories are about growing up and learning, whether in high school, like Kristian Bruun's story of boarding school bonding over comics and girls in "The White Glove Brigade," irritating lesbians online before realizing you are one in Gabby Rivera's "Trolling for Lesbos," or the tough choices we make in walking away from a relationship as an adult in love in Hope Larson's "Cosplay."

We have returning creators from *The Secret Loves of Geek Girls*, too! Tini Howard discusses how fanfiction warnings mirror her real life romantic history in "tinismessypast," Jen Vaughn shares the bonds built with strangers through the love of podcasts in "The New Gods of the Airwaves," Diana McCallum shares fifty very relatable anecdotes about being a geek in love, Cara Ellison and Maddie Chaffer rage against the hypocrisy of controlling women's sexual fantasies in "Women Love Jerks," and yes, even I share a story about learning firsthand the intersections of sex, respect, and career in "Pros at Cons."

And we were fortunate to have Margaret Atwood return for this volume, collaborating with Michael Walsh and Jordie Bellaire on "The Horror, The Horror," a story about the blurred reality of being a secret horror fan while maintaining the façade of a nice, sweet girl. Similarly, Gerard Way, collaborating with Robert Wilson IV and Kelly Fitzpatrick, shares a story about imaginary worlds—of the simultaneous peace and limitless excitement of living in your own head and balancing this with necessary human connection.

Here's the thing: we each have our own stories, unique to us. But they will always connect to someone else's story, as you can see through the connected themes between strangers' stories in this book. Your own personal story will connect in many different ways to several here, and in others you'll find new perspectives that will make you a more empathetic person. So I have an assignment for you. Find a friend—whether you sit down for a meal, or connect via DMs—and try sharing your stories together. You'll be surprised at how you can find joy in mutual connection.

FOREWORD

It occurs to me that I might seem an odd choice to write the introduction to an anthology of romance stories, considering that I am a middle-aged bearded dude whose personal life is largely organized around watching period mysteries on Netflix (*Miss Fisher's Murder Mysteries*, represent!), playing video games, and hanging out with my teenaged daughter. Admittedly, I did write a romance comic for Vertigo that was later the basis for the CW series *iZombie* (of course, I never told anyone at Vertigo that *iZombie* was really a romance comic, but it was), and interpersonal relationships have always played a big part in the stories I write. But when romantic elements work their way into my novels and comics, it's often less about the relationship between two characters, and more about a character discovering something about themselves, realizing who and what they really are.

Reading the stories in this anthology, I was struck by how many of them were as much about people gradually becoming themselves as they were about people finding someone to love. And there is such a refreshing array of different identities, orientations, and identifications on display here, which I think reflects positively on the times in which we live. As difficult and challenging as our world might be at the present moment, I would argue that there has never been a better time in recorded history for people to discover who they really are, for one simple reason:

Representation matters, and people find it easier to become who they are when they see themselves reflected in media and stories.

People my age love to complain about "Millennials." There is an entire cottage industry of think pieces about which industry or tradition millennials are supposedly responsible for killing next. Those articles are invariably patented nonsense, of course, and the criticisms about millennials are almost always completely baseless. But we shouldn't be criticizing millennials; we should be *thanking* them, because millennials are goddamned pioneers. Over the last few years, I've watched as young people on Tumblr and elsewhere online have blazed new trails in personal identity, exploring new ways of being and interacting with the world around them. Whole new categories of gender expression and sexual orientation are continuously being mapped out by these latter day Magellans, and the fact that all of it is being carried out in a public space means that other people who struggle with the same questions can follow the trails marked out by those that came before them.

It wasn't always like that.

One of my oldest friends in the world struggled with depression, anxiety, and self-doubt for decades, until the experience of watching a speech given by Lana Wachowski just a few years ago helped put a name to the well of unhappiness deep within—gender dysphoria—and put her on the path to eventually transition into the woman that she always really was. Now my friend Lilah Sturges, at the age of 46, is happier and more comfortable in her own skin than I've ever seen her before.

For my part, I have always been great at relationships, but not so much with romance. Newly single in my mid-forties after an amicable separation, I found myself having the same difficulties with dating that I'd had in college and again in my mid-twenties. I would meet women that I really enjoyed spending time with, but then things would fall apart when I realized that I just wasn't attracted to them. In fact, I've only ever been attracted to a handful of women my entire life, and even then only after deep emotional bonds had developed between us. I've fallen in love with women that I wasn't attracted to, but never been attracted to a woman I wasn't already in love with. It wasn't until last year when I encountered the term "graysexual" that I began to suspect that there might be something to that pattern, and when I came across a definition of "demisexual" on Tumblr, I realized that I was reading about myself.

My teenage daughter came out to me and her mother as a lesbian shortly before her thirteenth birthday (which, admittedly, was something I'd known about her for a long time, but I was glad that she felt comfortable sharing it with us), and I think that she came to that realization as young as she did in large part because she saw herself reflected in the media that she consumed. She could see gay and lesbian characters on screen or in the comics she read, and say, "Hey, that's me!" And when I see her with her friends at school—trans kids and gay kids and ace kids and on and on—all of them comfortable in their own skins, knowing who they are because they have seen models for who they could be in the media they've consumed and the online communities that they take part in, I can't help but wonder how things might have been different for people my age—for me, for Lilah, and for innumerable others like us—if we could have seen ourselves reflected in stories at that age, too.

Representation matters and stories are important, and I have to thank Hope Nicholson and all of the contributors to this anthology for sharing their own stories with us. I know that countless readers will see themselves reflected in these pages, and that it will make all the difference in the world for them.

—Chris Roberson
Portland, Oregon 2017

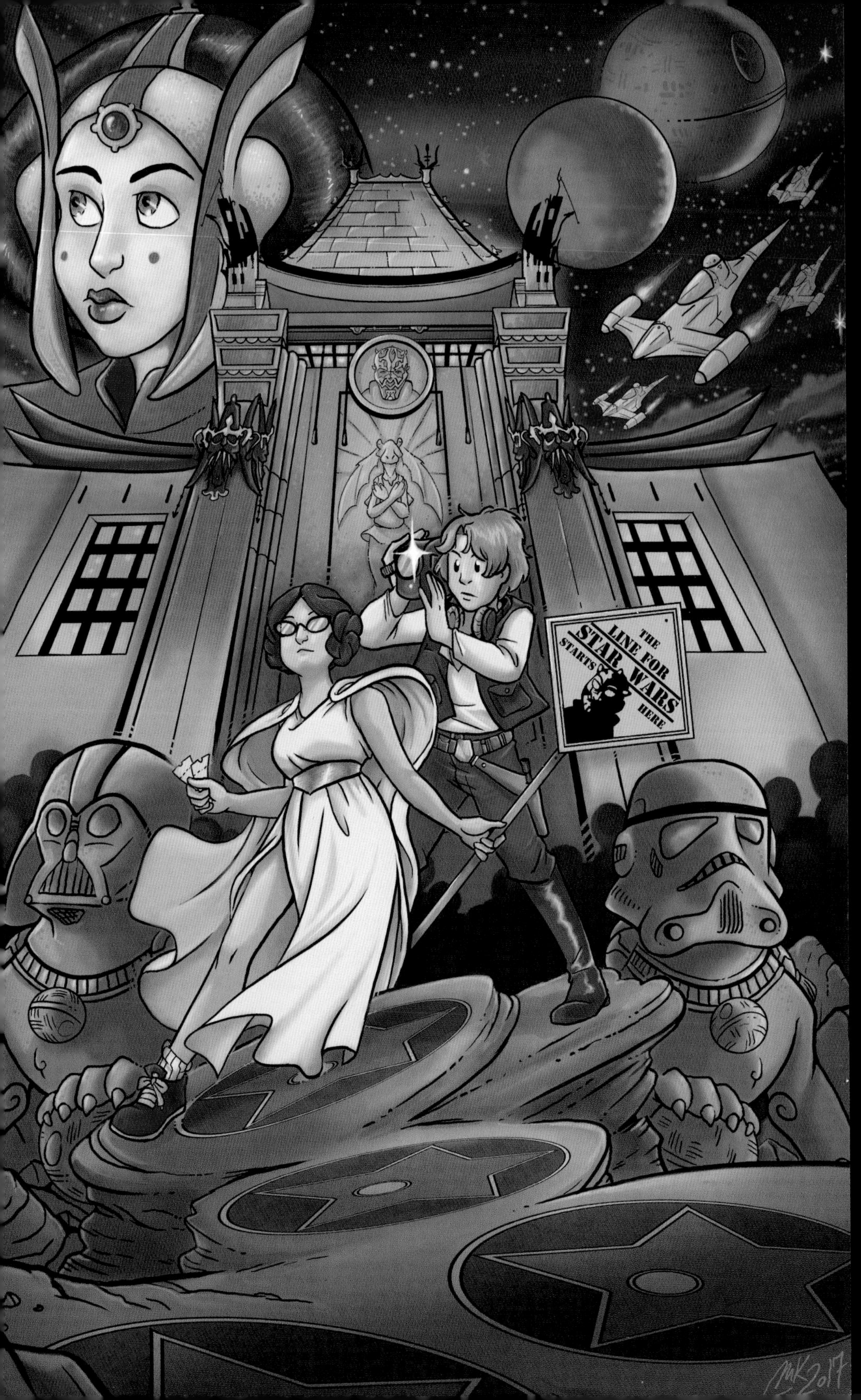
THE LINE FOR STAR WARS STARTS HERE

MY PHANTOM MENACE

Cecil Castellucci, illustration by Megan Kearney

The *Star Wars* line was just a little ways down from the Mann's Chinese Theatre in front of a parking lot. The first week there were just a few of us. Sitting on the sidewalk for hours with nothing to do but talk about *The Phantom Menace* and how good we thought it was going to be. Slowly, we made the sidewalk ours. With a world map with marks of the phone calls we received in solidarity with our camping out. A sign with Darth Maul's head that said *The Line Starts Here!* A banner for the Starlight Children's Foundation, which we were raising money for with our sit-a-thon. A modified street sign to press the button at the cross-walk that said *Use the Force.* There was a definite buzz in the air and what at first seemed like a strange thing to do slowly became *the* thing to do. We were creating our own microsociety and it was all centered around this thing that we loved. We were a ragtag team of Rebels fighting for the thing we loved, no matter how ridiculous it seemed to everyone else. Most of my friends didn't understand what I was doing or why. But they cheerfully visited me, bringing me food and books. Having a reason to be a looky-loo. And I would bet that they were secretly wishing that they could be that passionate about something. As though they didn't love *Star Wars*, too.

He arrived a week after me with his friend. He wore a blue shirt and green army pants and he was holding a DV camera, hell bent on making a documentary of the line. He was going to be a filmmaker, he said.

We were both cinephiles. Maybe I was more so than he was at the time, but I'm sure that he's caught up by now. We were both in indie rock bands. Both wore our hearts on our sleeves. We both loved *Star Wars*. We were both drawn to be on this sidewalk for six weeks at this time because we thought it would be magical. And it was.

What is it about *Star Wars* that hits the heart so hard? I think about it now and I feel so complicated. I love it so much and it will be in my DNA forever and I sometimes now get fatigued. I am so fiercely proud to be a small part of it and also I feel like I'm as far away as Luke felt living on Tatooine. It informed me and made me start on the path of becoming a storyteller and yet I am nourished by other things now. I am overexcited by it and I am over it. But of course I'm not over it. I never will be. Maybe the way I feel about *Star Wars* is the way I feel about him. Someone I will always love but someone that I will grow past.

That first week, before he arrived, I would sleep at the theater at night and work at IFP West during the day as a temp for the last week of my contract. So he was not the first boy that I slept next to. True story: I slept next to a murderer the first night. There were only eight of us out there and we were cold and we thought he was a street kid and we gave him Chinese food and let him spend the night. We huddled for warmth and then the next day we laid down the rules: raise money for the Starlight Children's Foundation, because that was the only reason we had a permit to live on the sidewalk, and do radio interviews on the constantly ringing pay phone. He did one interview and then left. He was weird. And likely poor and I felt bad about it, until the cops came later and told us they were calling him the Swedish Meatball Killer and he was on the lam and should be considered dangerous.

I had been enjoying my time on the line, but hadn't quite connected with anyone. These were my people but also not my people. Even though now I consider that merry tribe a part of my Rebel faction. We went through the Star Wars together and are bonded for life. And honestly I've seen them over the years but I haven't seen him since the last time I said goodbye, crying at an airport. But when he arrived with his best friend, I knew I had found the person that was closest to being cut from my cloth. They were my kindred spirits. It was an immediate recognition. Like when you look at someone and know that they are an old friend. Or like they are forever a part of your heart. He looked like Woody from *Toy*

Story. All legs and arms. His eyes were a beautiful blue green, the kind of eyes you dive into and swim in.

He always had that camera up, observing and filming, like he wanted to participate but maybe didn't want to at the same time. It was as though he was somewhat embarrassed. The camera giving him some psychic distance from being a nerd. There were concerns from others on the line about being viewed as nerds. *Star Wars* shirts were banned from the line. No lightsaber battles allowed. I thought it was ridiculous. We were waiting for *Star Wars* tickets. The accoutrements of nerdery were not what made us nerds. Our actions made us nerds. Being there made us nerds. Why is it that people don't want to be a nerd? Or that they didn't then? It seems like everyone is a nerd now. Everyone wears it like a badge of honor. No one would think it was weird to wait six weeks in line for a movie now. But then, the whole country was laughing at us for loving *Star Wars.* We were the butt of the joke in *FoxTrot*, on Leno, on the nightly news. *Good Morning America* checked in with us on a weekly basis. And then America would laugh. Remember, this was before smartphones and streaming, but eventually we had an online streaming of the line. We were being broadcast for all to see. There were many lines waiting for *Star Wars: Episode 1*, but we were the biggest, the longest, the one most made fun of.

Jimmy Kimmel came to the line and tried to cut as a joke. It was a bit to make fun of how nerdy we were. My boy got upset. He cried. He refused to sign a waiver so when it aired he's blurred, but there he is crying over Jimmy Kimmel who was dressed up as Yoda, saying that it wasn't fair. Maybe this was the first moment that I knew it wouldn't work between us. My boy was sensitive, maybe too sensitive. Or maybe it was being young? Something that I was moving on from.

I remember meeting him and having a running monologue in my head that repeated: Just kiss me. Kiss me. Kiss me.

He was twenty-four and I was twenty-nine, which seems like it's close in age and shouldn't matter but at that age, and in the end, it did. He was a boy and I was a woman. I was ready and he was not. In the way that I see all this now, that makes a difference.

I was invited to an IFP premiere of the film *Three Seasons* by Tony Bui and invited him as my date. Just me and him, eating free food and getting drunk. Holding hands for the first time. There was so much said and unsaid between us. Do you like me? Do you like me? Do you like me? We had that kind of first kiss where you breathe into someone. His mouth on mine like it had been there forever. Like his lips were meant to kiss mine. His arms pulling me in. That was the night I slept in his tent, because why would I leave once I had found him?

It took me a few days to move into his tent from the other tent I was in. I just wanted to be with him all of the time. This beautiful nerdy boy with a film camera. This beautiful nerdy boy who declared our little band of three a Team Tomorrow. This beautiful nerdy boy who declared that he was a gentleman and a scholar. This beautiful nerdy boy who loved to make things beautiful. He loved to present things in such a way that everything was always special. A plucked flower. An impromptu picnic. A perfectly prepared bed. These are things that I loved about him.

You should know that we pitched our tent on Lou Rawls's star every night. "You'll never find another love like mine . . ." I like to think that Lou Rawls would be happy to know that every time this boy and I made love on the *Star Wars* line we did it on his Hollywood star.

He and I would spend our time on the line making plans because we were in love. Life plans. We would get married. For sure. I would go to Texas with him. I had found my man. We got Queen Amidala tattoos, but in different places, declaring that we would get matching tattoos in the place that the other had it when we got married, instead of rings, because who needs a ring when you have two twinned hearts?

I still look at my Amidala tattoo and think of him. Of breaking up with him over the phone because I wanted him to make a plan to move to Los Angeles from Texas and not make a plan about going to Sundance. What about our future? What about the direction we were facing? Let us look further. Let us look toward forever.

One of us was the Rebel and one of us was not. I'd wager in the long run it was me. I loved us the longest while he moved from girlfriend to girlfriend to wife after me. I refused to get a day job, committing myself to all art all the time. I took the morning-after pill after a sloppy night so that I would get to write another day.

If I'm honest, I would get frustrated with him, because I was quick and he was slow. His heart so big and bold but he couldn't keep up with me. One thing that I would learn from this relationship with him is that I love a man with a brain that is quicker than mine. But I also know that a quick brain can sometimes come along with a cruel heart. Which is better? Honestly I don't know. No, wait. The heart. The heart. The answer is always the heart. Maybe I was the one that was cruel.

We decided that what we were on was adventure time. That we needed a team name and code names. He dubbed us Team Tomorrow because that's the direction that we were facing. He was Future Bird and I was his Lady Bird.

If he hadn't been there, I would have probably left the line. Given up on sleeping there every night for six weeks. I would have gone home sometimes. Taken more showers. Been at the back of the line instead of number eight. But how could I leave when I was in love? When nothing else seemed as important as him and *Star Wars*?

We would whisper about pop culture and about all the things that made us love the world of stories. I wish I could still be in that tent talking about the merits of Chewbacca and all the Topps playing cards and reciting *Raiders of the Lost Ark* word by word to each other.

The night the movie came, the theater let the first twenty of us go in and choose our seats. He and I held hands and took our seats and then they opened up the theater to everyone else. That was the best part of the movie for me, watching the masses rushing into the theater, waving their lightsabers, running to get seats. And the Lucasfilm logo coming up with all of the lighted lightsabers slowly waving as the soundtrack came in and we screamed.

I did not go to the Mann's Chinese Theatre to wait for *Star Wars: The Phantom Menace* in a tent for six weeks to fall in love. I went because I was so excited about a new *Star Wars* movie that I could not imagine not marking it in some profound way.

But six weeks of living on the street in a tent is exhausting. I was tired when the film got going. I was irritated that it was so late. I was worried about my relationship: What would happen after the film? What did our future look like? Adventure time was ending and reality was creeping in. Worse, the movie was like watching a thing that I couldn't understand. Was it me that was the problem? Had I outgrown this thing I loved? It seemed dumb and hard to follow. Taxes and an annoying kid. I kept trying to find that feeling that *Star Wars* had always given me and I couldn't find it. A horrible thought occurred to me: I am not enjoying myself. And then another thought after that: What if he likes this? If he did, I knew

I would have to break up with him. But instead, he leaned over in the middle of the movie and said, "This movie is terrible." And I answered, "I love you." Because in that moment I did. Forever and only him.

Six weeks with what *Star Wars* could have been, should have been. Now I wish the film had been better. Like it would have given us a better chance. But all that hope for what could be burst upon viewing. A thing that seemed in poster and preview like it could be good, could be bloated and boring.

Our meet-cute could have made a good story to tell at cocktail parties decades later. It would have been adorable. Along with it I imagine the two kids we would have had, nerds as well. My best-selling novels and his Sundance-worthy films. All the cool arty interviews we would do where we were a unit, two working artists in love. But it was never going to turn out that way. I couldn't live in Texas and he couldn't live in Hollywood. I really did write novels and I see him doing so well, but only living at the edges of film. I'm the Han Solo, the Princess Leia, the Darth Vader in this scenario. He's the Uncle Owen.

It was a pipe dream to think that we could make it after the streets. After a terrible movie. After having different kinds of ways of moving through the world. After having brains that moved at such different speeds. All I know is that I loved him with all of my heart even though he was not the one for me.

I haven't seen him in eighteen years. But my love hasn't changed. He will always be my Future Bird, the captain of my Team Tomorrow. I will always be his Lady Bird. And I like to remember us from a long time ago, in a galaxy far, far away, when we are holding hands while the whole country laughs at us for being nerds.

THE HORROR, THE HORROR :

Words - Margaret Atwood
Line work - Michael Walsh
Color Art - Jordie Bellaire

In high school I did a lot of babysitting.

The bedtime story, the warm milk, then right to sleep!

I'm sure we'll get on fine.

I told them stories.

And then Cinderella married the prince...

...and doves pecked out the eyes of the wicked sisters. The end.

I sang them lullabies.

♫ Hush, little children, Don't you cry ♫ Mama's gonna bring you a ♫ pecked-out eye ♫

Good night, sleep tight, don't let the monster under the bed bite.

I cast a spell on it.

I turned it into a bedroom slipper.

Let's hope that works.

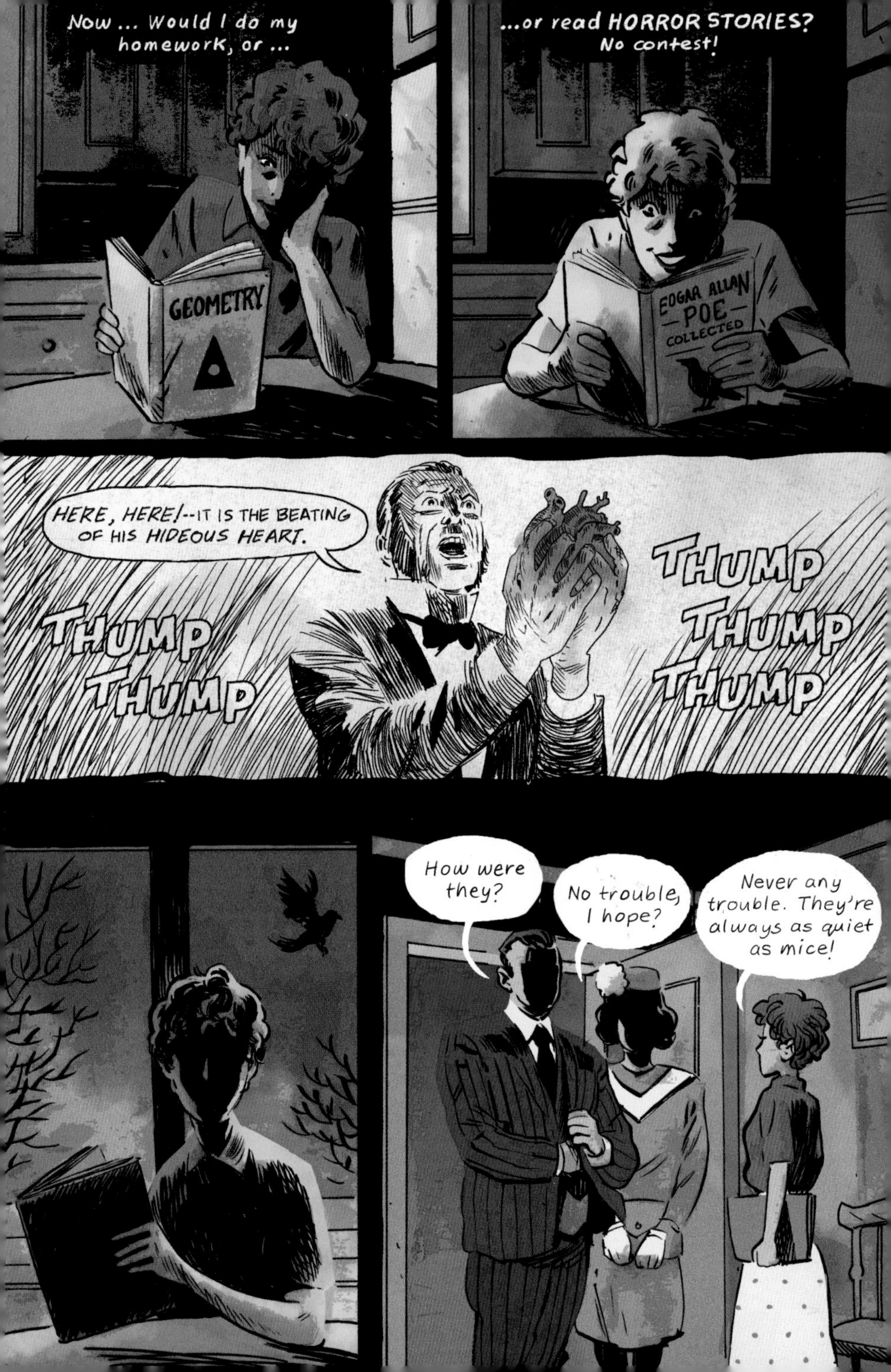
Now ... Would I do my homework, or ...
GEOMETRY
...or read HORROR STORIES? No contest!
EDGAR ALLAN POE COLLECTED
HERE, HERE!--IT IS THE BEATING OF HIS HIDEOUS HEART.
THUMP THUMP
THUMP THUMP THUMP
How were they?
No trouble, I hope?
Never any trouble. They're always as quiet as mice!

ghttime was write time...

She drank down the mysterious potion...

And was transformed into... Her Evil Twin!

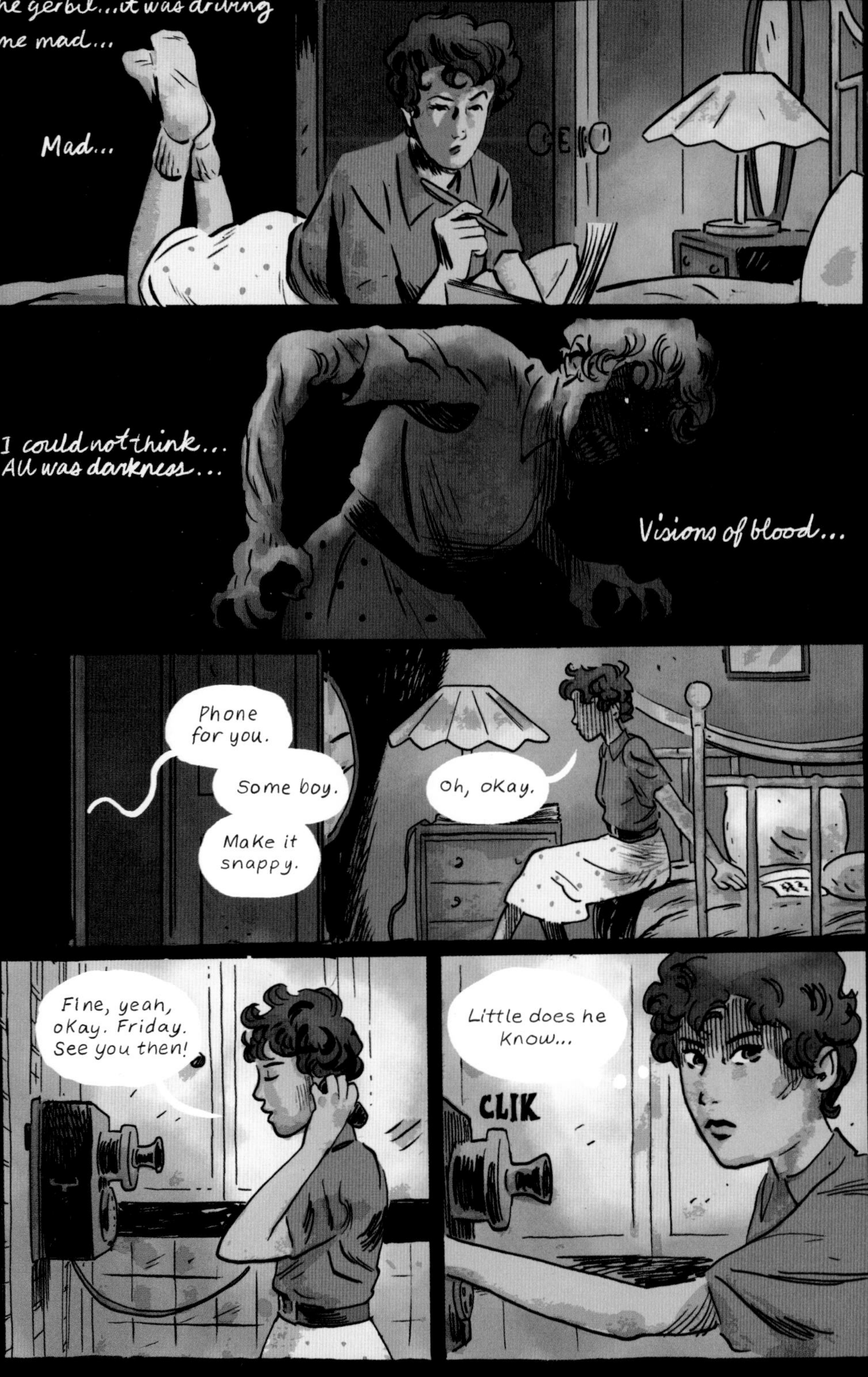
...the gerbil...it was driving me mad...
Mad...
I could not think...
All was darkness...
Visions of blood...
Phone for you.
Some boy.
Make it snappy.
Oh, okay.
Fine, yeah, okay. Friday. See you then!
Little does he know...
CLIK

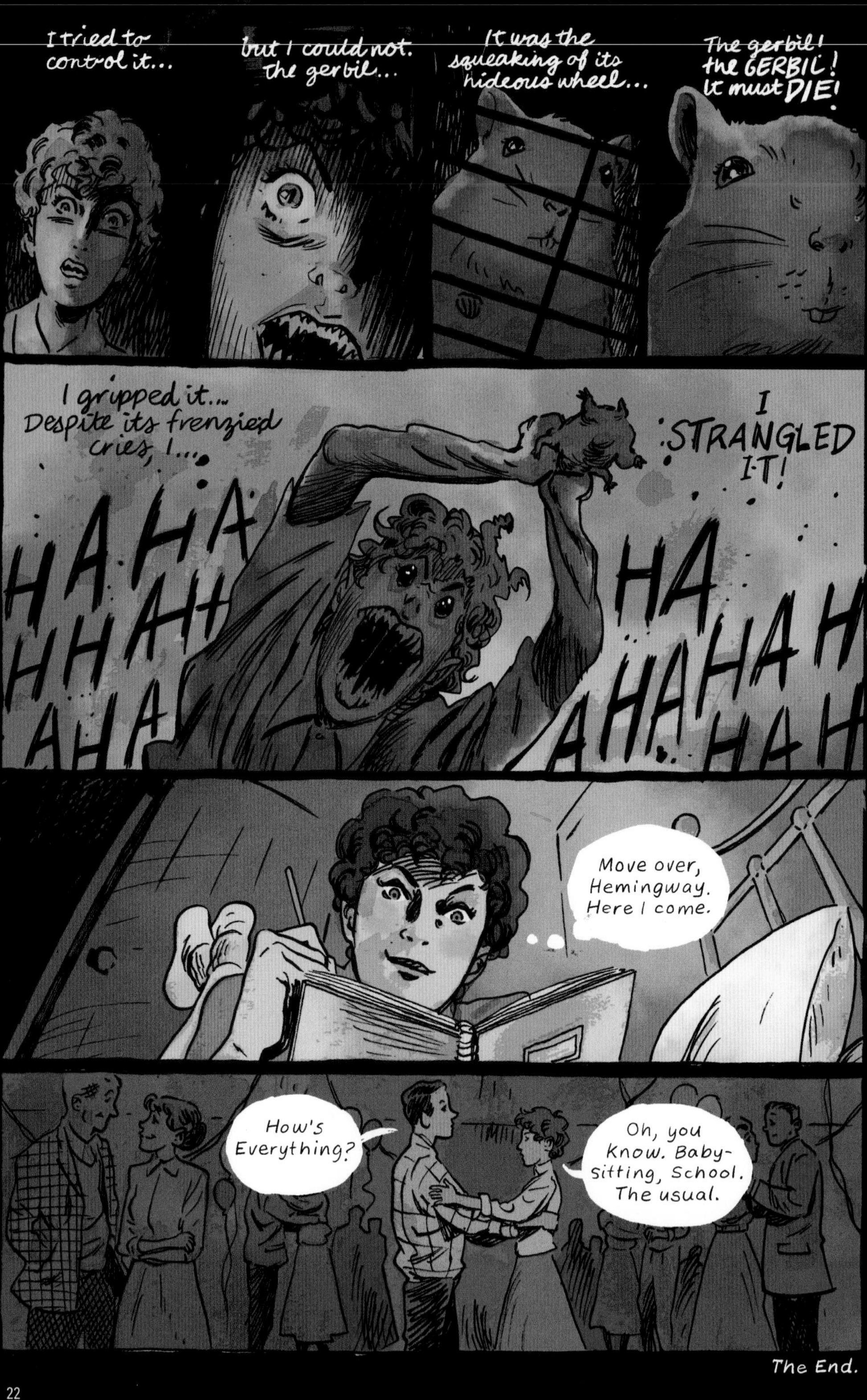
I tried to control it...
but I could not. The gerbil...
It was the squeaking of its hideous wheel...
The gerbil! the GERBIL! It must DIE!
I gripped it... Despite its frenzied cries, I...
I STRANGLED IT!
HAHAHHAHHAHAH
HA HAHAHAHAHHAHAH
Move over, Hemingway. Here I come.
How's Everything?
Oh, you know. Baby-sitting, School. The usual.

The End.

SMUDGED
BY LETTY WILSON

TEN MINUTES TO.

I GUESS WE SHOULD HEAD OVER...

SO WE CAN SET UP RIGHT AWAY?

YEAH.

WHY DID WE VOLUNTEER TO DO THIS?

I DON'T KNOW AAAAAA.

OKAY.

SQUEEZE

WE'RE BOTH NERVOUS. OF COURSE WE ARE. WE'RE ARTISTS, NOT PUBLIC SPEAKERS.

CHARACTER DESIGN FOR COMICS

BUT AS FAYE'S SPEAKING, HER VOICE WOBBLES JUST A LITTLE...

AND I WANT TO GO HOLD HER HAND. AND IT HITS ME THAT I'VE NEVER WANTED TO DO THAT BEFORE.

I USED TO DRAW ON MY HANDS AS A CHILD. MOSTLY AT SCHOOL, OR WHENEVER I WAS BORED AND HAD ACCESS TO A PEN.

I'M NOT SURE WHEN THE EYES STARTED BEING PART OF IT--MAYBE AFTER I SAW "PAN'S LABYRINTH"? I THOUGHT THAT MONSTER WAS REALLY COOL.

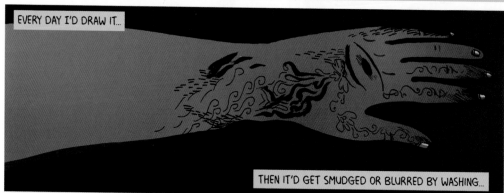

EVERY DAY I'D DRAW IT...

THEN IT'D GET SMUDGED OR BLURRED BY WASHING...

AND I'D DRAW IT AGAIN.

IT WAS SOMETHING TO FOCUS ON INSTEAD OF THE CONSTANT FEAR.

A SMALL ATTEMPT TO TRY TO PROVE I WASN'T INVISIBLE, THAT I WAS A REAL PERSON.

SOME TIME ALONG THE WAY IT BECAME A COMPULSION.

BY THE TIME I WAS AT UNIVERSITY I **HAD** TO HAVE A PEN IN MY HAND DURING CLASSES, **HAD** TO KEEP MY EYES DOWN, DRAWING.

I SPENT A LOT OF TIME ALONE.

Want to come tonight to wat Dr. Who?

SOMEWHERE AMONG THE VIDEO GAME PLAY-THROUGHS AND ONLINE RPGS I LEARNED A COUPLE OF NEW WORDS: **ANXIETY** AND **ASEXUALITY**.

THE FIRST OF THOSE I WAS AWARE OF, BUT HADN'T CONSIDERED IT COULD APPLY TO ME.

SEXUAL INNUENDO

ACTUAL SEX

WEIRD FLIRTING

SEXUAL INNUENDO

BUT ONCE I KNEW MORE ABOUT IT, SUDDENLY I COULD SEE IT TANGLED IN EVERY PART OF MY LIFE.

THE SECOND NEW WORD OPENED UP A WHOLE NEW PART OF MYSELF I HADN'T BEEN AWARE OF. I WASN'T BROKEN ANYMORE, COULD STOP WAITING TO GROW UP, WONDERING WHY I DIDN'T.

JUST LIKE THAT, I HAD A MAP. I COULD FIGURE OUT WAYS ROUND MY PROBLEMS, STRATEGIES.

BIT BY BIT, I STOPPED DRAWING ON MY HANDS. STOPPED NEEDING TO.

STARTED DRAWING FOR A LIVING-- OR AT LEAST LEARNING TO.

IN THE PROCESS, I FOUND PEOPLE IT DIDN'T HURT TO BE AROUND.

WHEN I WAS LITTLE, I USED TO WONDER IF I WAS CAPABLE OF LOVE. I WASN'T CLOSE TO MY FAMILY, BEING AROUND OTHER PEOPLE WAS TIRING AND STRESSFUL, AND THE IDEA OF A BOYFRIEND OR GIRLFRIEND WAS TERRIFYING. IT SEEMED LIKE IN ORDER TO HAVE ANY KIND OF RELATIONSHIP I WOULD HAVE TO CHANGE SO MUCH AS TO BE A DIFFERENT PERSON.

BUT LOVE ISN'T A SUDDEN, ONE-OFF EVENT.

IT GROWS FROM REPETITION. REPETITION CONFIRMED ME AS A PERSON, AS SOMEONE WITH FRIENDS SHE LOVES, AND WHO LOVE HER.

I WAS FINDING OUT THAT I WAS A REAL PERSON, AND CONTACT WOULD NOT SMUDGE ME.

A WEEK AGO.

I WANT TO BE NEAR MY FRIENDS. I'VE NEVER WANTED TO BE NEAR PEOPLE BEFORE. I THINK PART OF BEING ASEXUAL AND AROMANTIC IS THAT YOUR FRIENDS BECOME THE MOST IMPORTANT RELATIONSHIPS IN YOUR LIFE.

STOP POKING THE MEATBALLS AND GIVE THEM HERE.

THEY'RE SQUISHY.

FINE, I'LL PLAY WITH THE SPAGHETTI INSTEAD.

OKAY.

I STILL FIDGET--I SPEND ALL MY DAY DRAWING, SO OF COURSE WHEN I HAVE NOTHING TO DO WITH MY HANDS I'LL GET RESTLESS.

I STILL GET ANXIOUS.
I STILL WONDER SOMETIMES IF I'LL END UP ALONE.

I DON'T THINK SO, THOUGH.
I'M NOT INK. THE PARTS OF ME THAT SMUDGE AND GET REDRAWN ARE ONLY PARTS OF ME.

BEING THE SLAYER

Buffy the Vampire Slayer *and the Burden of Trans Girlhood*

Gwen Benaway

**SEASON 2, EPISODE 22, "BECOMING: PART 2."
ORIGINAL AIR DATE: MAY 19, 1998.**

BUFFY: Open your eyes, Mom. What do you think has been going on for the past two years? The fights, the weird occurrences . . . How many times have you washed blood out of my clothing, and you still haven't figured it out?

JOYCE SUMMERS: Well, it stops now!

BUFFY: No, it doesn't stop! It never stops! Do—do you think I chose to be like this? Do you have any idea how lonely it is, how dangerous? I would love to be upstairs watching TV or gossiping about boys or, God, even studying! But I have to save the world, again.

I was never allowed to watch *Buffy* as a kid. We didn't even own a television until I was twelve or thirteen years old. The only place I could watch TV was at my gookum's house in the summer or in the homes of other families. *Buffy* was satanic, filled with witchcraft and powerful women who slew demons and wore leather jackets. When I saw my first episode at a friend's house, I was immediately entranced by images of a petite blond girl fucking shit up in black boots and tight jeans. I wouldn't watch the entire show until I was in my early twenties, but that image of Buffy stayed with me.

When I started transitioning last year, I went back to *Buffy*. I watched the entire series again from the late '90s into the mid 2000s, when it ended. The first months of my transition were a living hell. I was fighting to get access to hormones while presenting in public full time. Facial hair removal was expensive and horrendously painful. Most of my close friends fell away, leaving me alone with time to spare. Work was accommodating, but I was regularly called by my old name or misgendered. It was one of the worst periods of my life. So it was Buffy and me most nights, retracing her journey through the images on the screen as I fought my own war.

I finally gained access to hormone treatment around six months into my transition. Pushing past the medical gatekeeping, I began the process of transforming my body and mind. I quickly realized that hormone treatment, while magical in its effects, was no easy road. Emotions skyrocketed and spun every day. Dark moods swept over me at work, lingering for days and driving me to close my office door. My doctor gave me no warnings or even explanations of what would come. I relied on the internet and the collective wisdom of other trans girls to understand what was happening to me. To put it mildly, I went a little crazy. I'm still a little crazy as my body and mind adjust from a lifetime of testosterone and switch over to estrogen's soft glow.

Buffy was an anchor. I would play *Buffy* in the background while I scrolled through Instagram and Facebook, watching everyone else step into their lives effortlessly. The feeling of being cut off from the world because of your gender is a deeply personal and profound one. People who haven't lived with some kind of difference in their life don't fully appreciate the pain of being denied access to the world because of some fundamental part of you. I didn't choose to be a trans girl. I just am one. This is the link which I began to see between myself and Buffy.

Buffy, as I'm sure most people know, is a vampire slayer. She is not just a vampire slayer, but the only Slayer for most of the show. She is a girl trapped by circumstances beyond her control. She is brought to the Hellmouth, a portal underneath her hometown, to save the world over and over again. Her powers are a supernatural strength and agility, but mostly she saves the day through willpower and raw brute force. The constant story arc of *Buffy* is her struggle with the destiny forced on her, the burden of being the Slayer. All Buffy really wants is to be a regular girl with a normal boyfriend doing typical girl things. She is a cute femme who wants to wear ponytails in pink tank tops. She ends up covered in blood at the end of every episode.

It's hard not to see the trans-girl connection in Buffy. It's impossible for me to not see my story in her story. No one has ever asked me why I transitioned. They've asked me about everything from my genitals to my surgeries to incredibly violent inquires about my gender identity, but not why I transitioned. I guess they assume they already know the answer. I wonder what they imagine in their heads about my transition, the narrative they construct around my transness. The truth is my transition was inevitable since my birth. I was born into this transness. Before I had words for what I was, it was already defining and shaping who I was and what I wanted. I couldn't escape transitioning. It had to happen. One day I would wake up and tell the world who I was. One day I would start my life over. The question was when.

Buffy doesn't have a choice as well. She is born into being the Slayer. Her adolescence until high school is normal, but she always felt different. She didn't know her destiny would be killing vampires, but it was always there, lurking in a graveyard and waiting for her. Throughout the show, she fights against the weight of being a Slayer. She tries to go to prom like a normal girl but ends up abducted and fighting off a horde of vampires. She tries to date an old friend from elementary school and he betrays her to a pack of vampires who try to kill her and her friends. She joins the cheerleading squad but discovers one of her fellow cheerleaders is a witch who kills her rivals. In other words, everything Buffy does or wants is in direct conflict with her destiny.

This extends to Buffy's love life. Throughout the show, Buffy tries to have a regular relationship with men. Her first love is a four-hundred-year-old vampire named Angel. He has a soul but loses it several times in their relationship. She can only see him at night because he can't walk in the sun. Her mother can't know about this relationship. She hides it from friends at first but eventually Angel becomes an ally in her war against evil. Their entire relationship is bound by the restrictions of her role as a Slayer and Angel's life as a vampire. Even when she tries to find love, Buffy is trapped.

My love life is similar. I dated bisexual men before transitioning. I think this was how my transness defined me before I knew what it was.

I liked being in sexual and romantic spaces with bisexual men because my gender didn't matter as much. With gay men, I needed to be a man at all times because femininity was undesirable. With bi guys, I could be their girlfriend. I could be as feminine as I wanted because they had an appreciation and desire for women as well as my current genitals. They were more willing to embrace me because they had worked to embrace themselves.

Many of my boyfriends called me by female terms of endearment. Our sex was profoundly gendered. I was often forced into the role of being the active partner in anal sex, but I still found more space in our bonds than in the gay relationships I should have been having. Gay men have never liked me, I assume because they could tell on some level that I wasn't a boy. Bi men have always been drawn to me. I think this is because we inhabit the same duality, a similar erasure of some parts of us in public while we negotiate a private desire. There is a major stigma against loving bi men, not unlike the stigma of dating vampires, because they're seen as inauthentic. Written as closeted gay men or straight boys who will fuck anything that moves, bisexual men have to carry the burden of society's judgment. Like me, they're always explaining themselves.

Buffy faces another problem in her love life that I connect with. She is the Slayer, an incredibly powerful woman who regularly stands up and fights for what she believes in. As much as she wants to be a regular girl, her life has made her strong and confident in ways other girls don't understand. There is a moment where the queen bee of her high school talks to Buffy in the hallway and tells her that she doesn't understand why Buffy is so weird. It's not like you're ugly, the queen bee says, but there's something wrong with you. Buffy's destiny has forced her to inhabit her power as a woman fully and it changes her.

In romance, Buffy is often stronger than her partners. They help her achieve her goals in various ways but they usually let her down. She saves them from themselves over and over again. Even when she wants to be soft and vulnerable with her lovers, she is forced to be the heroine. She becomes harder and harder as the show progresses. Every time she tries to connect past her role as the Slayer, she is snapped back to the reality of saving the world. Her lovers struggle with her power. They resent her for how clearly she sees the world. They walk away when she needs them. She has to do it alone, every time.

Since I transitioned, love has been complicated. As my body and face change, I move closer to more feminine presentation but it's a slow journey. Being seen as a girl is often dependent on your appearance. I've learned that I occupy some strange middle ground in most people's minds. Half a girl, a sorta girl we use female pronouns for, but a girl without the full rights or access of other girls. It is the most lethal and violent part of being trans. I used to believe that people in my life would eventually see the real me and embrace me as her. I don't believe that anymore. I will only be a girl to the outside world when I fully look and sound like one. This is violence, but I've learned not to struggle against it anymore.

I want to be free and wild in my gender. I try to escape my destiny but it always finds me. Like Buffy, the closer I get to people, the more they hurt me. No matter how much I trust them, they always slip up and let me see how my girlhood is in question to them. I'm always looking for a way out of myself. I wonder how much my dynamic with men is my fault. Do I expect them to save me and carry me into the other side of life? Do I force them to occupy certain roles in my life while erasing who they are? I think I just want to be seen fully and embraced in the wholeness of myself. There's a reason I pick bisexual guys to love. They usually want the same acceptance I do.

Like Buffy, I hope for a love which lets me exist as myself without compromise. The truth is that I don't hate being trans. I hate what the world forces me to do in order to prove my humanity, but I like being a trans girl. I feel powerful in my body as a trans woman. Buffy has the same struggle. She is happiest and most at ease when she is saving the world. When she is beating the fuck out of demons and twirling through the air with a sword in her hand, she is complete. What hurts her is the inability to be all of herself: the badass who defeats evil and the girl who wants to cuddle. This is the deepest pain I have ever felt. When am I whole?

Early on, Buffy tries to date an old friend from elementary school. He betrays her because he secretly is trying to become a vampire. The episode ends with her burying his body in a graveyard with her Watcher, the show's father figure. She asks her Watcher if life ever gets easier, a question I've asked many older trans women since I transitioned. He looks at her and gently answers, "What do you want me to say?" Does life get easier, do the bad guys always dress in black, and do the good guys always win? No, he tells her, you will always be the Slayer. This will never get easier.

There is a moment at the end of *Buffy* which I love. In the final episode, after an apocalyptic battle where friends die and her lover is killed, Buffy leads the surviving friends out of the destroyed town. She has saved the world again and so completely that it doesn't need to be saved anymore. The Hellmouth is destroyed and her town is obliterated. Her mother died several seasons ago. In other words, this is the moment where Buffy is truly free from her destiny. For thirty-five seconds in the camera's frame, Buffy is just a girl like any other girl. What does she do with this moment?

She looks at the camera. She pulls her lips into a firm smile and sets her eyes on the horizon. She radiates the quiet strength which has always defined her. She tells her friends to walk forward, to go on. She reconciles the pain and loss through her courage. She does what she has always done throughout the show. She demonstrates a fundamental humanity and power. She is still the Slayer, even if the world doesn't need saving. She is the Slayer because she is more than her destiny. In other words, she transcends herself to embrace the parts of her which separate her from the world. They are what makes her capable of responding to the crisis around her.

Buffy is a trans girl. We do this every day. We do it when friends and lovers let us down. We accept the misgendering and the pain of surgery. We go on. We embrace the parts of ourselves which keep us back from the world. We forgive lovers to chase our own hearts. We are weary, but we do the work. I love this in myself and in other trans women. I make so many mistakes, but I try to balance the burden of my destiny with the girl I am. It is never easy, but it is always mine. Slayer, tranny, heroine, savior.

I think of Buffy in that final shot whenever I doubt myself. I think of her when I walk past leering men. I imagine her leaping up and kicking a vampire whenever I defend myself. I become the Slayer. I acknowledge my power. I save my world, again. I don't want to, but I will. Like Buffy, I am the Chosen One and no matter how hard I fight, I won't be free of it until my world ends. What happens to Buffy when the last shot ends? Where does she go and what comes into her life? Does she ever find a love worthy of her?

I don't know, but I know whatever comes, Buffy will be okay. This is her power. The courage to keep fighting through denial and rejection and loss, to overcome hopeless odds, to be heroic when everyone else is giving up. She doesn't want to do this, but she does because it's what she is. I'll be okay as well for the same reasons. The truth is Buffy and I are not normal girls. We want to be, but everyone in our lives knows we aren't. They see the strength in us even if they can't embrace it.

But what is more feminine than fighting for your humanity? Men have their humanity handed to them. It's preordained. Women are the ones who fight to make our way and work to have our partners respect us. People praise the sweet girl but they never acknowledge the bitch who gets shit done. So here's to Buffy, a complex and powerful woman in a world of paper-thin girls. You're my inspiration.

Women I LOVE Jerks

WRITTEN BY CARA ELLISON & ILLUSTRATED BY MADDISON CHAFFER

HAH, HE'S NEVER AVAILABLE WHEN I WANT HIM. HE'S ALWAYS LATE AND NEVER HAS ANYTHING TO SAY. HE'S DATING SOME OTHER GIRL THAT HE LIKES BETTER.

SO WHY ARE YOU SLEEPING WITH HIM? HE SEEMS LIKE A JERK! YOU'RE A FEMINIST!

WELL... BECAUSE I LIKE TO HAVE SEX WITH PEOPLE I'M ATTRACTED TO.

ORGASM VIA HETEROSEXUALITY

full sex to completion WITH A HUMAN MAN ISN'T SOMETHING THAT HAS TO TEACH WOMEN ABOUT THEMSELVES. ATTRACTION IS JUST ATTRACTION. BUT SOME FORMS OF ATTRACTION ARE ALSO SHAPED BY OUTSIDE FORCES.

STOP THAT.

STOP WHAT?

MEN WITH INCONSIDERATE BEHAVIORS TOWARD WOMEN ARE VENERATED AND ADORED IN WESTERN CULTURE. IN FICTION, THESE MEN ARE OFTEN WRITTEN BY MEN, WITH A MALE AUDIENCE IN MIND.

TAKE *STAR WARS*'S HAN SOLO. HAN DOESN'T RESPECT LEIA'S BODILY AUTONOMY ALL THAT MUCH. (I THOUGHT THIS WAS ROMANTIC WHEN I WAS A KID.)

35

OR TAKE JAMES BOND IN THE CONNERY YEARS.

WHERE WAS I? AHH YES...

GHUH!
= STAB

WINK

BUT OH, HE'S SO *heroic* AND *handsome*

OR HEY— ANOTHER HARRISON FORD CHARACTER, INDIANA JONES.

HELLO, MARION.

I WAS YOUNG! I WAS IN LOVE! IT WAS WRONG AND YOU KNEW IT!

OUR FAVORITE MALE HEROES CONTINUALLY TAKE WHAT THEY WANT FROM WOMEN WITHOUT ASKING.

WHEN MEN ARE AGGRESSIVE TOWARD YOU IN [ci]TY, IT'S OFTEN FRIGHTENING, UNWANTED, AND [trau]MATIZING. AND WHEN WE SAY WHAT WE [...] WANT, WE ARE OFTEN PHYSICALLY [and] SOCIALLY PUNISHED.

MEN ARE ALSO SUBJECT TO THE WORLD TRYING TO TELL THEM WHAT THEY SHOULD FIND ATTRACTIVE ABOUT WOMEN. IT'S A MINEFIELD FOR EVERYONE OUT THERE.

BUT ALL THOSE INCONSIDERATE HEROES WERE WRITTEN BY MEN, FOR MEN. WHAT HAPPENS WHEN WOMAN AUTHORS TAKE CONTROL OF THE TOXIC FANTASY MAN?

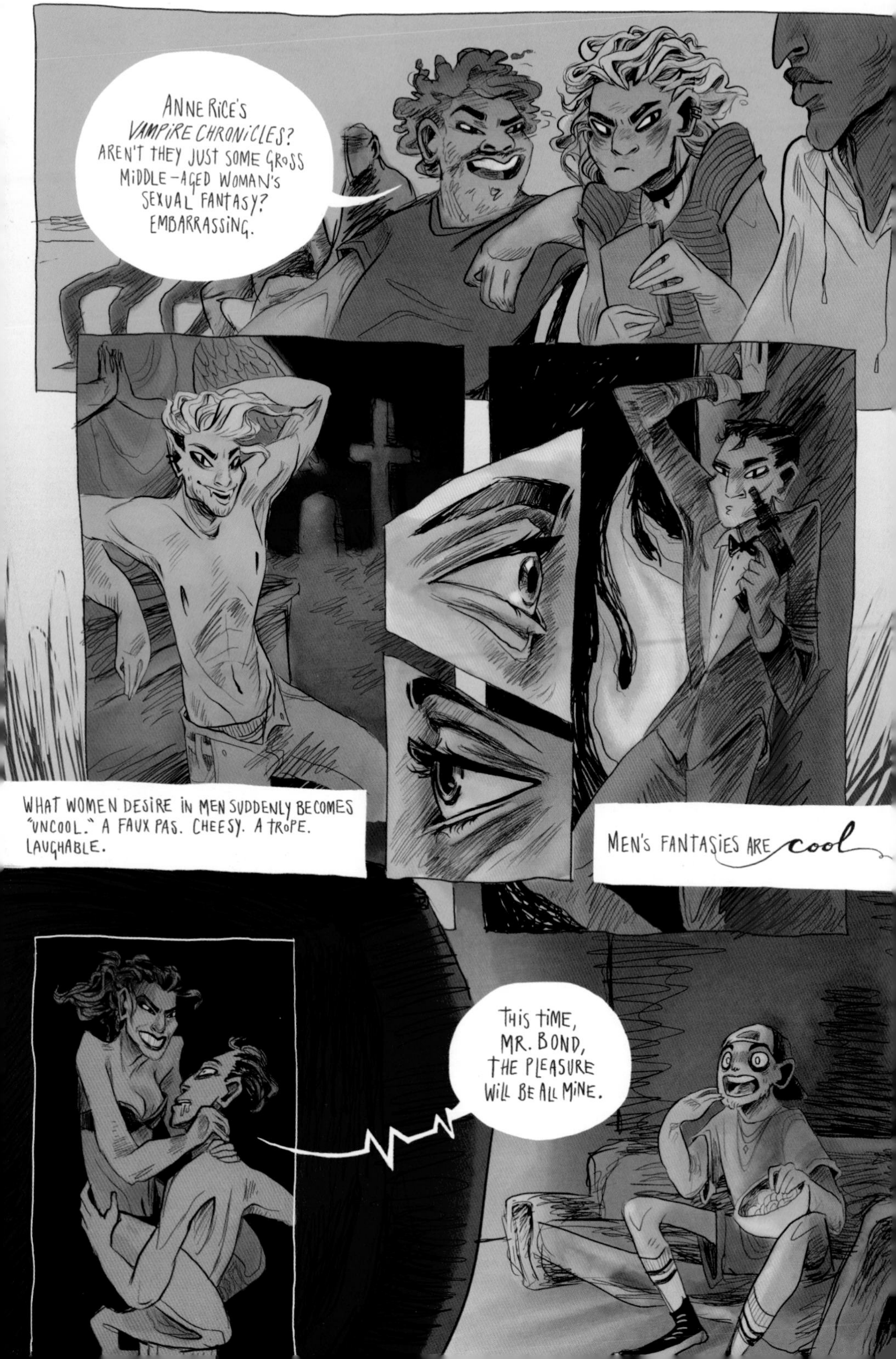
ANNE RICE'S *VAMPIRE CHRONICLES*? AREN'T THEY JUST SOME GROSS MIDDLE-AGED WOMAN'S SEXUAL FANTASY? EMBARRASSING.
WHAT WOMEN DESIRE IN MEN SUDDENLY BECOMES "UNCOOL." A FAUX PAS. CHEESY. A TROPE. LAUGHABLE.
MEN'S FANTASIES ARE cool
THIS TIME, MR. BOND, THE PLEASURE WILL BE ALL MINE.

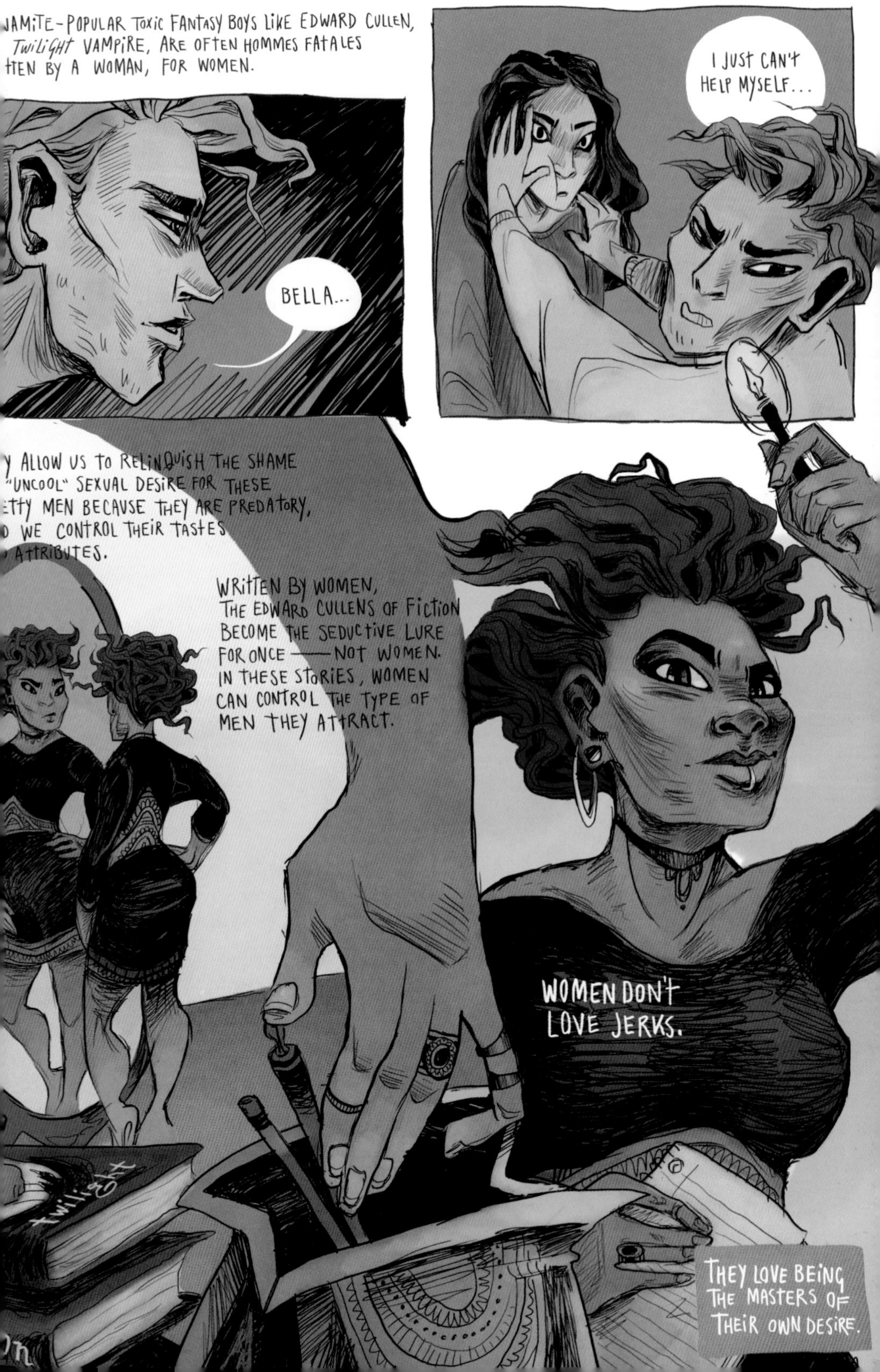

JAMITE-POPULAR TOXIC FANTASY BOYS LIKE EDWARD CULLEN,
TWILIGHT VAMPIRE, ARE OFTEN HOMMES FATALES
TTEN BY A WOMAN, FOR WOMEN.
BELLA...
I JUST CAN'T HELP MYSELF...
Y ALLOW US TO RELINQUISH THE SHAME
"UNCOOL" SEXUAL DESIRE FOR THESE
ETTY MEN BECAUSE THEY ARE PREDATORY,
D WE CONTROL THEIR TASTES
ATTRIBUTES.
WRITTEN BY WOMEN, THE EDWARD CULLENS OF FICTION BECOME THE SEDUCTIVE LURE FOR ONCE —— NOT WOMEN. IN THESE STORIES, WOMEN CAN CONTROL THE TYPE OF MEN THEY ATTRACT.
WOMEN DON'T LOVE JERKS.
twilight
THEY LOVE BEING THE MASTERS OF THEIR OWN DESIRE.

Do you feel it?
by Shee Phon
You're so cute.
UM!
Um, I dunno how to kiss.

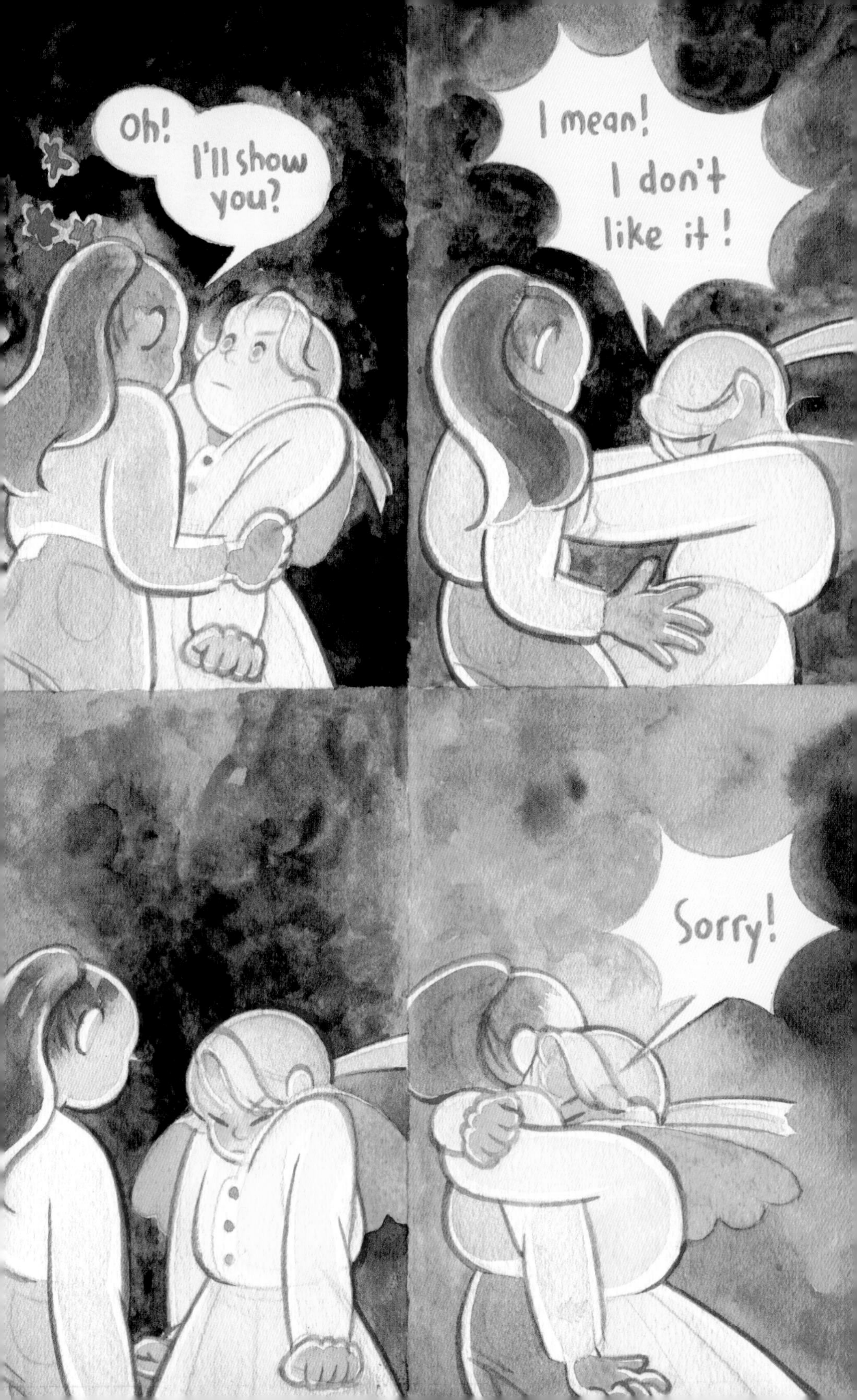
Oh! I'll show you?
I mean! I don't like it!
Sorry!

Do you feel it?
Feel what?
NOW?
OW!
OW!
HEY!
It's okay if you don't wanna kiss me.

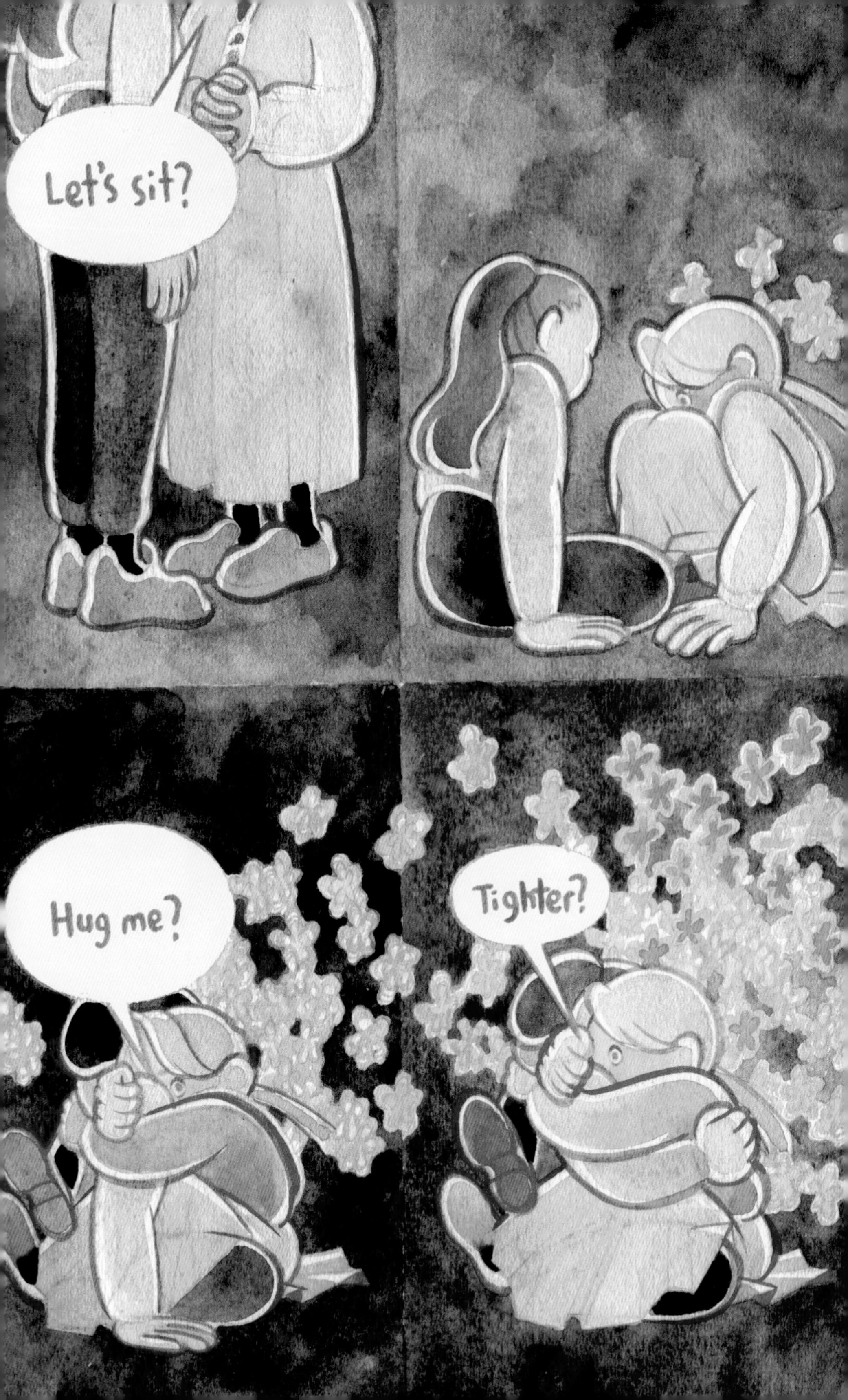
Let's sit?
Hug me?
Tighter?

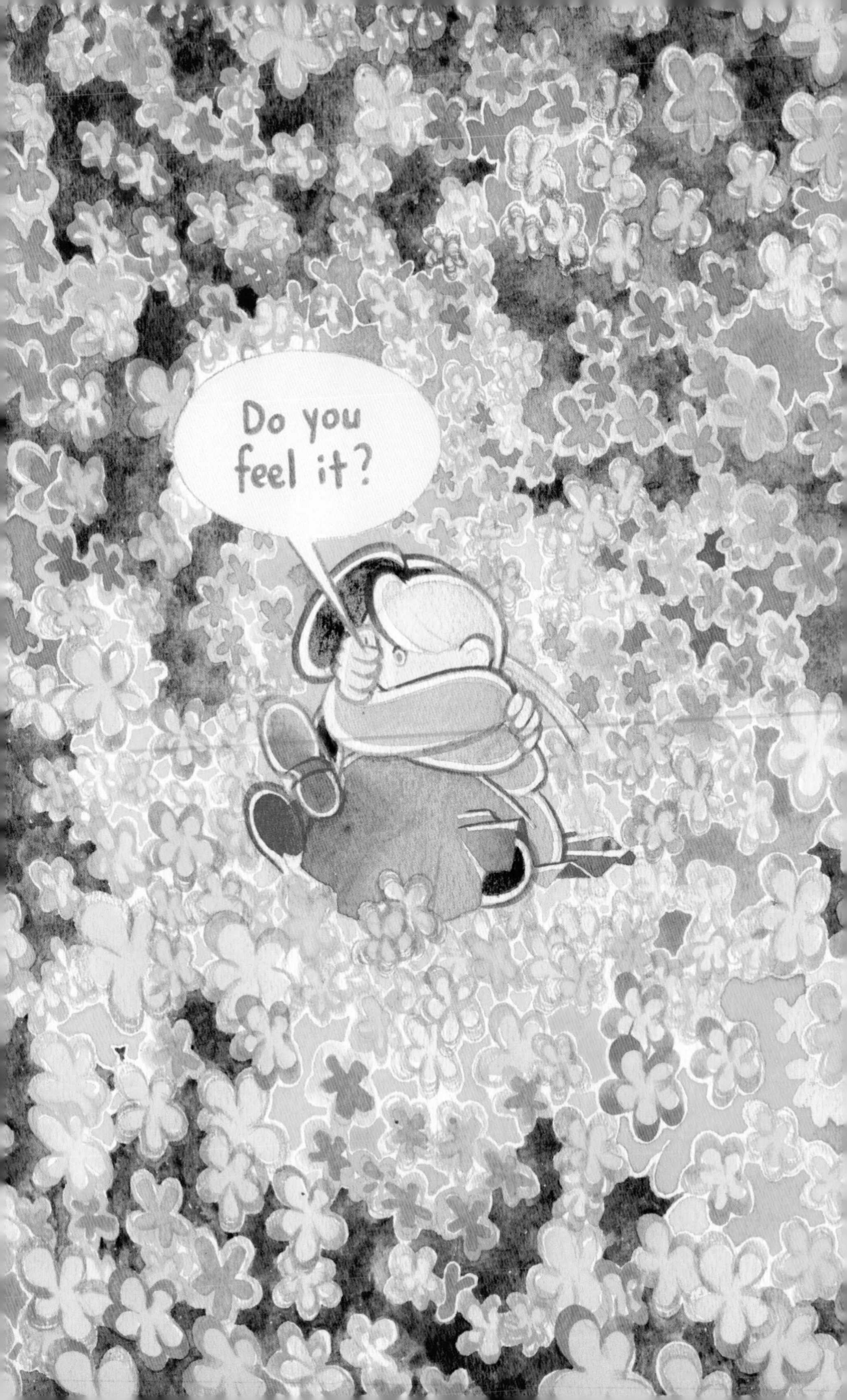
Do you
feel it?

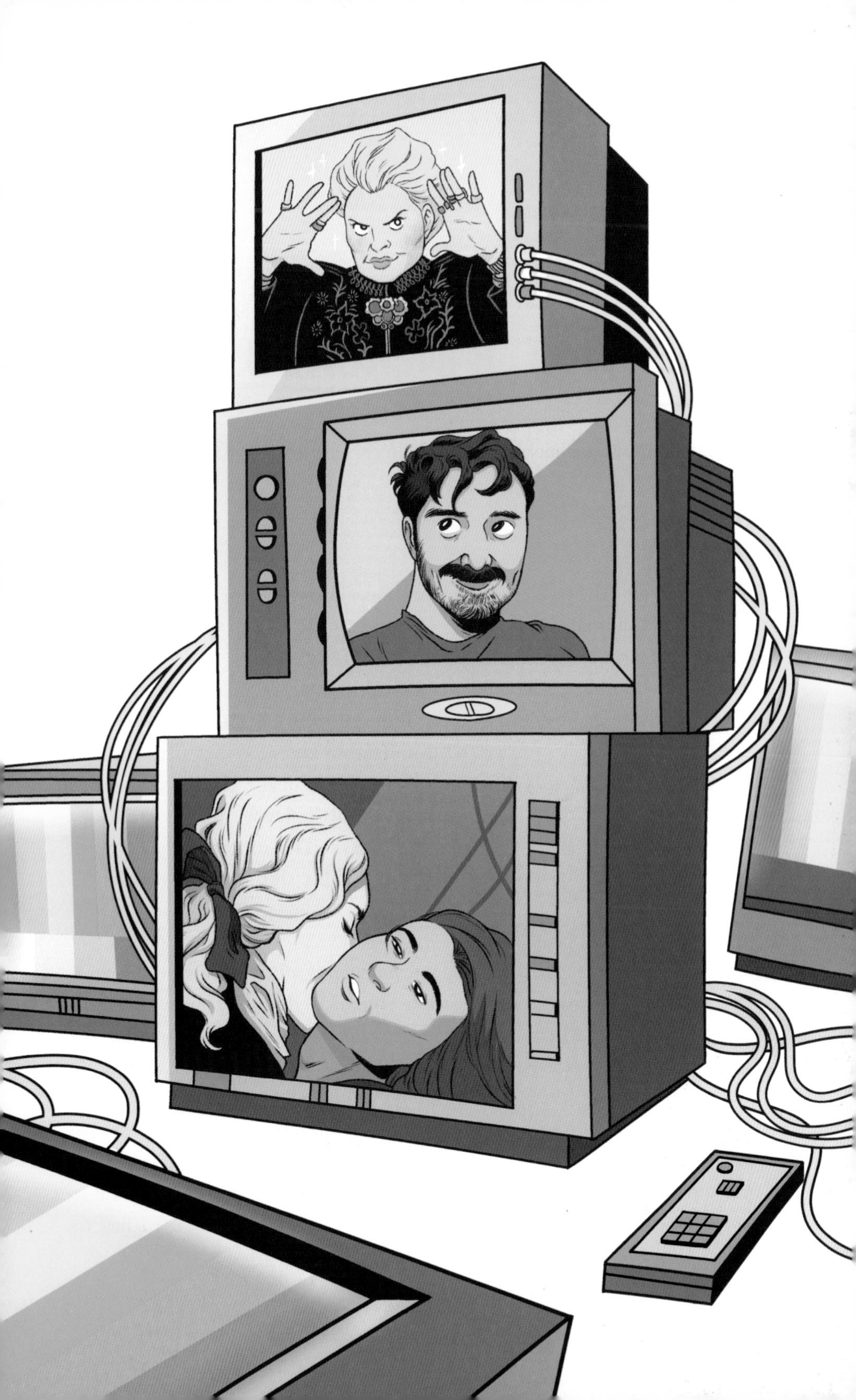

THE WALTER MERCADO EFFECT

Ivan Salazar with thanks to Andi Santagata, illustration by Maddi Gonzalez

Tom Cruise's lithe face emerges from the shadows, fangs out, hissing like a predatory animal. Descending on a prone Brad Pitt, Cruise sinks his teeth into the downed man's neck. First, only enough to see the teeth pierce skin and blood flow, but then Cruise's lips seal around the wound, pressing firmly against Pitt's neck. The music swells and with it Cruise and Pitt rise into the air, locked in a deathly embrace meant to quench the thirst of both men's hungers for blood and death. And it's here that something shook loose in me—watching Pitt's sleepy, dreamy stupor at the man draining his life with a "deep kiss." The moment Cruise took his lips away and Pitt let out a brief but audible sigh, a warm realization washed over me.

THIS. IS. HOT!

If you haven't guessed (or have never seen it) the above scene is from the 1994 blockbuster horror (slash romance) film *Interview with the Vampire*, and as far as I've tracked, it's also the exact moment where I was—as Brad Pitt put it—"born into darkness," a.k.a. my first significant queer realization.

But this moment—this origin—wasn't something that was always known to me. Hell, it took me a couple of decades to really dust it off and examine it as something akin to a queer awakening. And in plotting a line from then to now, I found that there was a LOT of dusting off I had to do. I had years of moments, experiences, and feelings that I'd overlooked, buried, and—in some ways—conditioned myself to ignore.

I was born Mexican. First generation in the US, to immigrant parents—and while sometimes they surprised me with how progressive they could be, that doesn't mean the Latinx culture I was surrounded by shared my parents' best ally days. When faced with questions of ambiguous sexuality in my family and in the surrounding Latinx culture, I felt like queerness was often a world that could be seen—could be heard, even secretly admired—but was never discussed or acknowledged.

But how do hot vampires fit into this?

Record scratch

Growing Up on TV and Movies

I grew up in a family of seven with four older sisters and after school it was common to find a few hours where I was pretty much alone in a house with access to bootleg cable with all the channels. So beyond watching what my parents thought I was watching, I'd peruse channels like HBO and Cinemax, experiencing movies and shows like *RoboCop*, *Akira*, *Hellraiser*, *Aeon Flux*, and tons of other media I probably shouldn't have been watching at age twelve. And through these completely blown-out and exaggerated examples of the human condition I started to piece together a sense of more complex human emotions, like morality, and possibly most impactful for me—sexuality.

Flipping through premium cable in the midnineties, I'd easily land halfway through a sex scene. Action movies had them, horror movies usually had them, and even comedies had pretty raunchy sex scenes meant to satirize their more serious film brethren. If you haven't seen the "sex" scene in *Hot Shots!* it's pretty damn ridiculous, but it's how I learned using ice cubes in foreplay is a thing—not that I knew what foreplay was at the time. Anyway, back to hot-vampire-related stuff.

It was on one of these solitary afternoons that I saw Tom Cruise's lips firmly pressed against a stupefied Brad Pitt's neck. As I stared at the screen with eyes wide, those images beamed into my brain and in those moments as they lifted off the ground something stirred. I didn't completely know what it was, but it felt familiar. A similar kind of excitement that stirred whenever a woman partially or fully nude flashed onscreen in those R-rated movies. It was attraction. It was want. It was need.

Something about that embrace between Cruise and Pitt made me want (and continue to want) to be in a similar situation—enraptured in an embrace, with someone tenderly or aggressively taking their mouth to my neck, making me theirs. To this day, I instantly melt into a puddle if there's any intentional or romantic touch that graces my neck—leaving me to only react with a brief but audible sigh.

But at the age of twelve and outside of the pejorative remarks hurled across the schoolyard I couldn't tell you what it meant to be "queer." And I definitely couldn't make sense of why this scene between two men captured my attention so much. This became all the more confusing when growing up I observed a Latinx culture that could use sexual ambiguity in media without acknowledging the real people and potential sentiments of queerness these people represented.

Growing Up Brown and Curious

Growing up brown, I had no nuanced idea of what queerness meant. I had no frame of reference within my family, and in terms of the Latinx media my family and I consumed, the biggest touchstones for anything resembling queerness were a musician named Juan Gabriel, a TV medium named Walter Mercado, and a Latinx theater my parents took me to sometimes, Teatro de los Pinos.

In my memories of the shows I went to at Teatro de los Pinos, the MC was almost always a drag queen decked out in sparkling dresses, fantastical wigs, and stunning makeup—she appeared as a confident, vibrant woman who kept the audience in stiches all night between skits, and there was never any questioning of her place leading the show. I couldn't tell you her name but I remember her as funny, bubbly, raunchy, but never too risqué. Sometimes the MC would flirt with the concept of an ambiguous sexuality, letting the voice deepen to a gruff man's voice for a punch line, reminding the audience through this blue humor of the man under the dress.

Those double-entendre theatrics straddled a line in their fluidity. A malleability of gender and sexuality that in the context of those performances was not only accepted but also celebrated. But that context was very limited. Those shows were purely entertainment, and if they meant to represent a potential vision of queerness, it was always in a nonserious way that made immigrant Hispanic families feel at ease and without cause to question. It was all part of the show, after all.

I can't remember if I ever asked my parents why the MC cross-dressed, though if I had, I know that it would have been played down by saying he was acting or that it was only a costume. And that was the interesting crux of trying to discuss or acknowledge anything outside of the heteronormative in the Latinx culture I grew up with—it just wasn't (isn't) discussed.

As I tug on this thread of memory, an immaculately coifed TV medium springs to mind. He dispensed astrological advice with a calm and welcoming kind of ambiguity around his sexual orientation that was easy to accept without having to question.

Helping set the dinner table as a teen in the mid-nineties, I remember the TV playing in the background, usually on a grisly Spanish news show, *Primer impacto*. As I'd set out the placemats, dinnerware, and glasses it was common to see at the end of the show Walter Mercado, a golden-haired, cosmically dressed mystic, give his daily advice on how to live your life spiritually and what the future held for each zodiac sign. This always struck me as the oddest break from *Primer impacto*'s usual coverage of strange natural disasters and *chupacabra*, UFO, and religious sightings, as well as the rise of cartel murders, which spared no gruesome details. It was during Walter Mercado's segments that the tone of the entire show shifted dramatically. He would appear on the screen with immovable blond hair and shimmering robes, against a backdrop of rotating religious and mystical iconography—crystal balls and gemstones one episode, Egyptian statues the next—and he'd empathetically speak to the audience at home in his sage, dulcet tones.

Ask most people growing up Latinx and they'd tell you Mercado was a household name. His luxurious, glittering outfits, calm and insightful demeanor, outrageous makeup, and perfectly sculpted hair made him shine with a visibly cosmic aura. And at the time his signature sign-off, "*Con mucho, mucho, mucho amor,*" was readily quoted by my parents, family members, and even kids at school. But how and in what way this sign-off was quoted was interesting to note. Imitations of this sign-off could be playful, acknowledging his over-the-top delivery of astrological musings, or venomous and used in the context of saying someone was as "gay" or "faggy" as Mr. Mercado.

The thing is, as far as I know, Mercado's sexuality was never confirmed. I'd read an article saying that he was "spiritually bonded" with a woman and business partner some years back. But at the height of his popularity—and in my household—his sexuality was not a topic ever up for discussion outside of jokes. And it's this that's an indicator of how Latinx families deal with the concept of queerness—a kind of willful ignorance. This is true even when it comes to larger-than-life Latinx celebrities—if there's ever a blurred line on their sexual orientation, there's no examination, only acceptance of what's displayed on the surface and discarding any notion of digging deeper. This felt especially true in the case of the legendary Mexican musical icon Juan Gabriel.

After the death of Juan Gabriel in September 2016, I listened to an NPR report where a panel of commentators discussed the subject of Gabriel's notoriously ambiguous sexuality. They talked about it being an "open secret" that was in a way acknowledged by fans worldwide but never discussed openly. They cited this willful ignorance of queer discussion as very Latinx, and called it the "Walter Mercado Effect."

The inimitable Juan Gabriel was Mexico's own version of Elton John— but even this might be a reductive way of thinking about Gabriel's legend. He was an orphan turned prostitute turned singer/songwriter turned actor turned international sensation. He sang rancheras as easily and as well as he did pop, disco, honky-tonk, and more. He earned the respect of *machos, mujeres, niños,* and *gringos.* And since the seventies he'd rocked stadiums the world over with his bedazzled mariachi outfits, eccentric charisma, and androgynous good looks. He was definitely a staple in the soundtrack of every house party and family gathering throughout my life and was even played recently at a wedding for a Latinx friend. Gabriel was and is still embraced as a true son of Mexico and yet one of the aspects about him most shrouded in mystery was his sexual orientation.

Even upon his death there was never any confirmation of Gabriel's sexuality. He himself would consider it terribly rude if asked outright in interviews. He once responded to this question by saying, "Things you see, you shouldn't always ask about." And I imagine it was that kind of repression that made it okay for the *machos* to love him, for the *mujeres* to dream about him, and for the *niños* and *viejos* to revel in his eccentricities—by never having to accept all of him.

I think about that when I think about the confusion I felt over that scene in *Interview with the Vampire*. Part of it being that these kinds of feelings toward the same sex were never discussed—they could be seen, heard, and even admired, but when it was at your doorstep asking you to face it and accept it, ignoring it was usually the best course of action for everyone. So though that "deep kiss" between Cruise and Pitt exploded something in me, growing up after that moment I didn't know what it meant. I felt like I was asked to not question it—and if I'd ever felt those same sex feelings toward anyone in real life, I was equally reluctant to do anything about it.

Growing Up Uncertain and Silent

Recently, I went on a date with a man—my first date with a man, actually—and as we sat in a courtyard in downtown LA eating ice cream we reached a point in our conversation where I said I'd be completely honest about anything he wanted to know. So he dug into the question I knew might come up.

"So you've never dated a guy?"

No.

"Ever messed around or anything?"

Nope.

"Ever kissed a guy?"

Nuh-uh.

I felt like this would be the thing that would immediately end the date. I worried so much about being seen as a tourist, someone just looking to see what it's like, someone not worthy of his time because—who was I? This novice just venturing out into the world of same-sex romance.

Although I'd never done the things he'd asked with another man, that didn't mean I hadn't had moments where I wanted to—where I felt like I could have if only I wasn't so unsure what those feelings meant.

In high school I was part of an educational enrichment program that took underrepresented minorities from several different schools and gave them college-level classes, tutoring, and summer courses at universities. One summer I made friends with a lovely boy who was funny and charismatic, with beautiful eyes and the impressive beginnings of a mustache. The entire summer there were times where I felt like our gaze lingered a bit too much on each other, especially when we went swimming in pools and lakes. During outings and movie nights we'd gravitate toward each other, even though we both had more familiar friends from our respective schools we could've hung out with. Seeing him interact with everyone I knew, I admired him, his easy nature, intelligence, and ability to get along with anyone—but there was more than that.

There were also the beginnings of attraction. Everything in me told me that didn't make sense. In the same way the moment between Pitt and Cruise didn't make sense—the way it stirred feelings inside me I couldn't or didn't want to understand. How could I possibly be attracted to a boy?

"I think I just like him a lot as a friend. That's it. Nothing more," I thought.

The summer would come and go without anything happening.

There was a time after that summer when we were finishing up our senior year and everyone from my summer program wanted to meet one last time before breaking off to our respective universities—and possibly never seeing each other again. It was then I saw that boy again. With his handsome smile, tight shirt, and even *more* impressive mustache, he told me how much he missed me, and that he wanted to hang out. He gave me his phone number and told me to give him a call to figure out when we could meet up. He hadn't mentioned hanging out in a group, or bringing along any of our more familiar friends from each other's schools. It felt like he just wanted to spend time with me and me alone.

I never called him.

And I don't know what became of him.

It's stupid what potentially good things fear can keep you from. Looking back, I know I was afraid. Afraid of what might've happened. Afraid of what I may have wanted to happen. Afraid of who would know. Afraid of what would be discussed or not discussed, but known and kept as an untouchable secret.

I was doing what I had learned to do when faced with any questions of sexual ambiguity—I buried them, didn't discuss them with anyone or even myself. What I'd learned from how the world treated that MC,

Walter Mercado, and Juan Gabriel I turned inward—and accepted the parts of myself that conformed to what was "normal" while keeping silent about anything that wasn't. That is, until the last few years.

Growing Up

But really, WHAT does all this have to do with hot vampires?

Over a year ago I ended a nearly decade-long relationship. It upturned my world and left me in a state I didn't recognize. Since then I've had to take a close examination of the events and experiences that linked together in my past to make sense of my present and use that to attempt to plot out a future. But immediately after it happened I felt like I was on my own—emotionally, mentally, and physically stranded. It was a frightening freedom that made me conjure up images of blasting out of an airlock into the star-studded black, with nothing but a spacesuit and a finite supply of air. But it wasn't long before fear turned into a sense of exploration.

Feelings of queerness were among many feelings that until the breakup existed only as abstract thought—repressed and put on a shelf marked "not for you, not now, maybe not ever." In the past year that frightening freedom has allowed me to learn to push past the tendency to willfully ignore my own feelings and desires—to have open discussions with myself and with others about queerness, empathy, and vulnerability in a way I hadn't experienced growing up.

With the aid of friends who stuck around as well as new friends and romantic partners, I've had help in normalizing my fledgling feelings of queerness. They let me begin to understand emotionally and physically what queerness means to me. And for that, and them, I'm eternally grateful. Just in the same way I'm grateful to Tom Cruise and Brad Pitt, the hilarious Teatro de los Pinos MC, the sage Walter Mercado, the inimitable Juan Gabriel, and the beautiful boy from that high-school summer. These people and memories from the past as well as friends and lovers in the present have helped me understand and shed a restraint of silence on my heart.

FIRST LOVES

Story by Amy Chu
Art by Valentine De Landro
Colors by Kelly Fitzpatrick

MASSACHUSETTS INSTITUTE OF TECHNOLOGY CAMBRIDGE, MA

I FIRST LEARNED TO LOVE AT MIT.

ARGUABLY THE GEEKIEST SCHOOL OF THEM ALL. I HEAR IT'S ABOUT 50/50 MEN AND WOMEN NOW. BUT I WENT AT A TIME WHEN THERE WEREN'T A WHOLE LOT OF WOMEN.

SO GUYS WERE ALWAYS THERE, READY AND WILLING TO ASSIST...

HEY, AMY, NEED HELP WITH YOUR PROBLEM SET?

UH, NO, NOT REALLY.

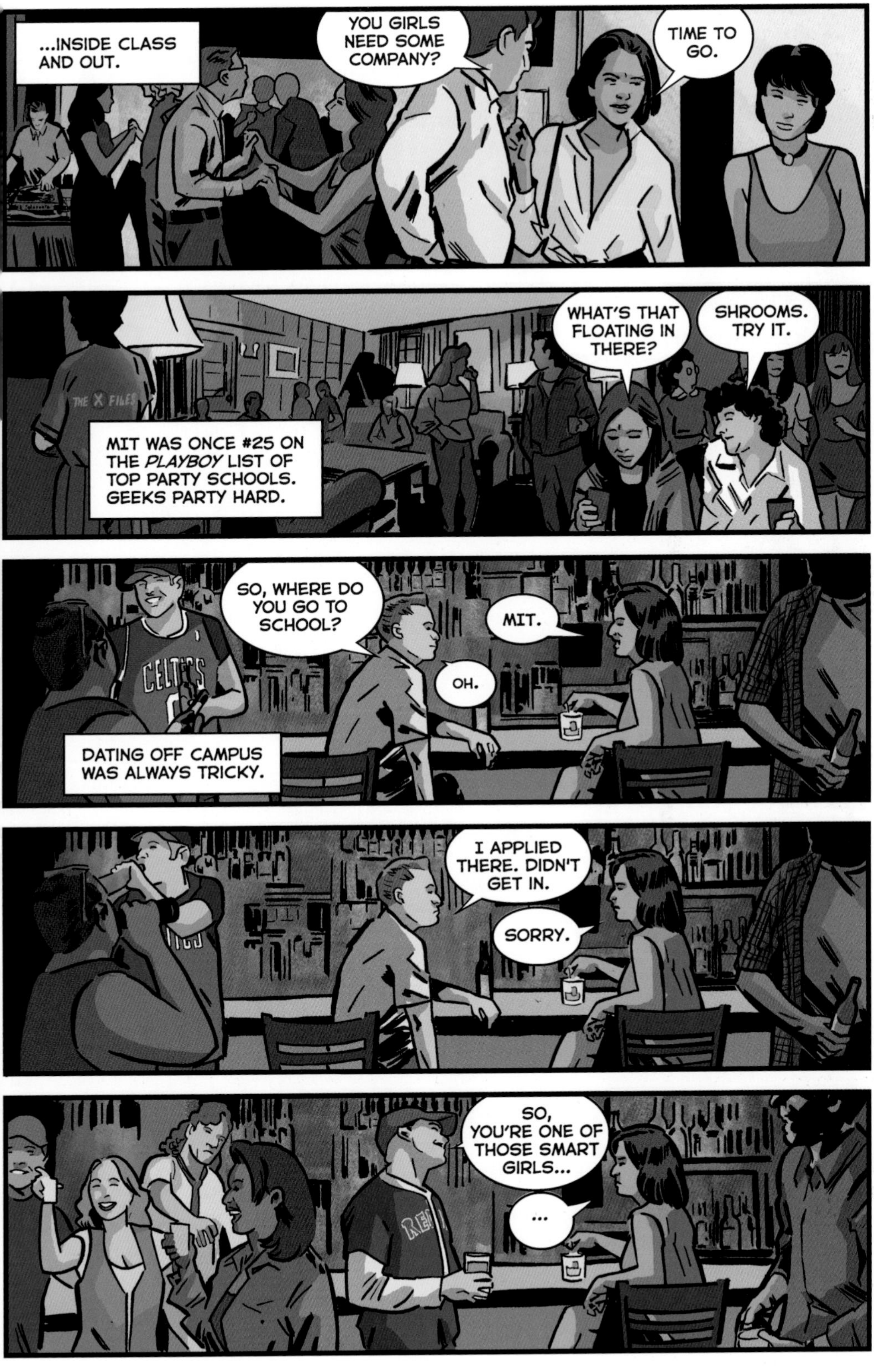
...INSIDE CLASS AND OUT.
YOU GIRLS NEED SOME COMPANY?
TIME TO GO.
MIT WAS ONCE #25 ON THE *PLAYBOY* LIST OF TOP PARTY SCHOOLS. GEEKS PARTY HARD.
THE X FILES
WHAT'S THAT FLOATING IN THERE?
SHROOMS. TRY IT.
DATING OFF CAMPUS WAS ALWAYS TRICKY.
CELTICS
SO, WHERE DO YOU GO TO SCHOOL?
MIT.
OH.
I APPLIED THERE. DIDN'T GET IN.
SORRY.
SO, YOU'RE ONE OF THOSE SMART GIRLS...
...

BUT THEN I FOUND MY SECRET LOVES OUTSIDE THE CLASSROOM...

I LEARNED BANK SHOTS AND BACK SPINS AND HOW TO HUSTLE THE SNOOTY FINALS CLUB GUYS DOWN THE STREET...

I GOT TUTORED BY SOME SENIORS ON HOW TO PICK LOCKS.

SOMEONE HELPFULLY WROTE A PAPER ON THE SUBJECT.

PE WAS MY MOST HATED SUBJECT, BUT AT MIT YOU COULD TAKE PISTOL, WHERE YOU SHOT .22s.

I TOOK THAT CLASS TWICE.

AND THEN THERE WERE COMICS. EVERYONE READ THEM.

THERE WAS EVEN A COMIC BOOK STORE IN THE STUDENT CENTER.

MY WORK/LIFE BALANCE SOLUTION WAS TO CRAM EVERY SEMESTER.

IN THE END I DID MANAGE TO GRADUATE, MUCH TO THE RELIEF OF MY PARENTS (AND ME).

LOOKING BACK I CAN HARDLY REMEMBER A THING FROM MY CLASSES.

BUT I DO REMEMBER MY FIRST LOVES.

AND NOW, HERE I AM, SEVERAL YEARS LATER, WRITING COMICS PROFESSIONALLY.

IF THAT ISN'T A HAPPILY EVER AFTER STORY, WHAT IS?

On the surface, we're a normal-ish "straight" married couple.

If I get groceries while you work on the car, are we succumbing to gender stereotypes?

We can switch any time you want.

We cannot. I suck at car.

DECEPTIVELY NORMAL.
by Dana Simpson

So we get asked the normal married-people questions.

How'd the two of you meet?

People seldom actually want to know in detail, so you can get away with vague answers.

We were in college.

Oh.

But it would be fun to answer in detail more often.

Let me transport you back to the 1990s internet.

Okay.

The first thing you have to know is that I was a "boy" at the time.

"I mean, I knew I was actually a girl, but I thought I'd never be able to tell anybody about it."

YEP I SURE AM A BOY I'LL JUST BE OVER HERE BEING A BOY THEN

"I was in high school when my household got that new thing, the 'internet.'"

You've got mail!

Dude! It's like freakin' STAR TREK.

"And it wasn't that long before I discovered MUCKs."

It was a role-play format. It stood for "Multi-User Chat Kingdom."

You whippersnappers.

"This is the part where I out my younger self..."

"Kind of a 'furry.'"

Yeah, I know. Shut up.

Although the fact that I kind of find that a more embarrassing admission than "I used to have different genitals" seems to represent a kind of progress.

If you think about it.

"'Being' a character who wasn't human gave the fact that I wasn't being my 'real' gender a bit of...plausible deniability."

I'm trying all KINDS of things! So it totally isn't that I'd rather be a girl in real life, no sir.

random guy

"And one day I met this seagull."

Hi.

Hi!

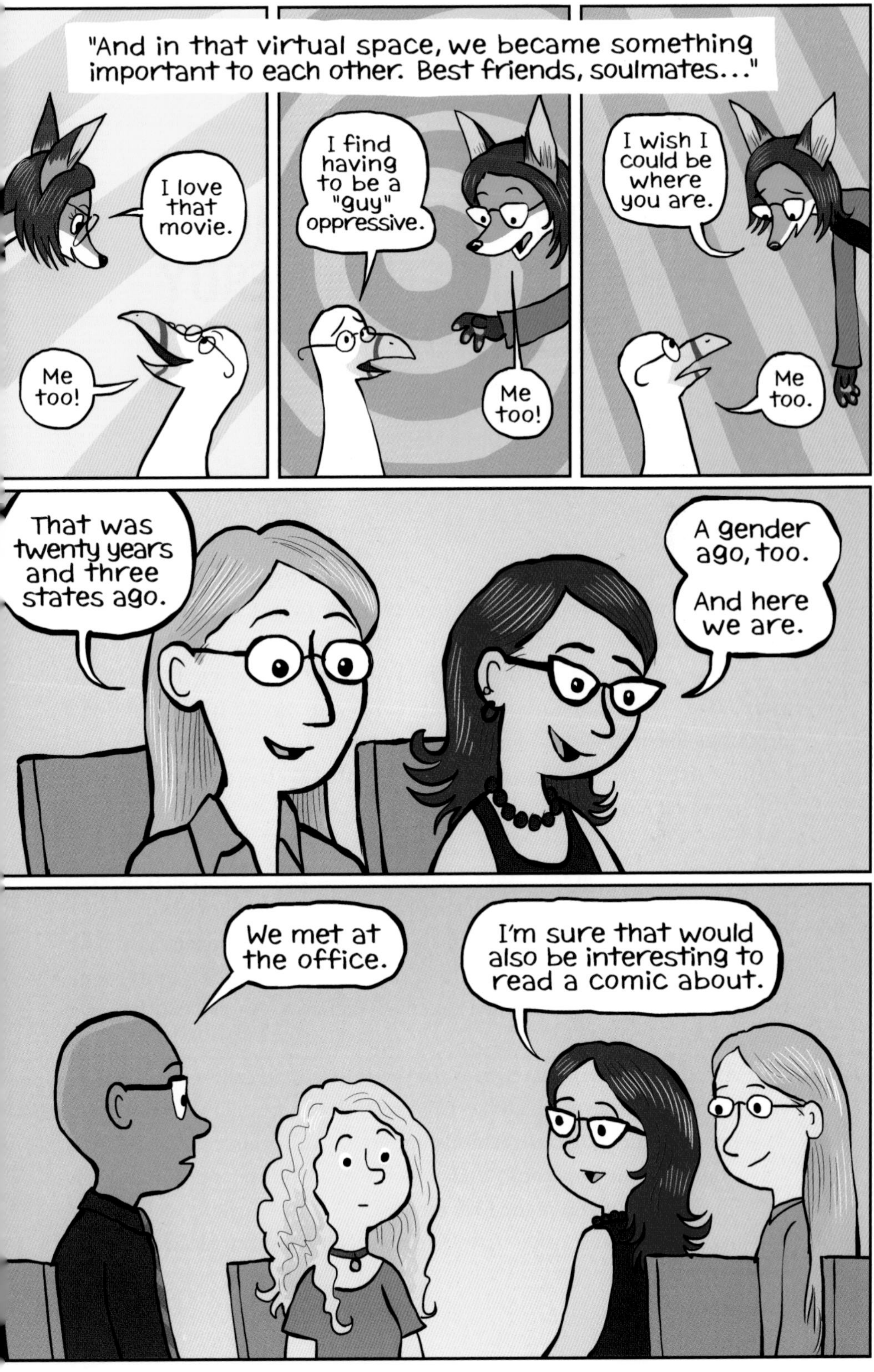
"And in that virtual space, we became something important to each other. Best friends, soulmates..."
I love that movie.
Me too!
I find having to be a "guy" oppressive.
Me too!
I wish I could be where you are.
Me too.
That was twenty years and three states ago.
A gender ago, too.
And here we are.
We met at the office.
I'm sure that would also be interesting to read a comic about.

THE 50 WEIRDEST THINGS THAT HAPPEN IN NERDY RELATIONSHIPS

Diana McCallum

Every relationship is different. They all have their quirks and intricacies, but something special happens when two (or more) nerds fall in love. Nerd-on-nerd love is like having a true partner in crime, the most comprehensive of soulmates. They are the Willow to your Tara. The Troy to your Abed. The Leslie Knope to your Ben Wyatt. Nerds in love just don't do things like the fandom-less folks of the world do. So if you find yourself in a nerdy relationship, here are a few things that may happen that you won't experience anywhere else.

1. You never argue about politics, unless you count your heated debates on the ethics of the Mutant Registration Act and the Sokovia Accords.

2. You've both learned a lot from science fiction. That means you have established code words to prove you're human in case of a body swap, robot duplicate, clone, or alien-takeover scenario. And if you haven't, you should.

3. If anyone asks if you have plans for the future, you can say yes because your zombie-apocalypse plan has been relentlessly strategized over.

4. When it comes to your relationship, you have to figure out which of you would be the superhero and which would be the sidekick. Oddly enough, neither of you is the love interest.

5. Cheating on each other is watching a Netflix show alone that you started together.

6. Yes, it's still cheating if it's a *Buffy* rewatch.

7. Spicing things up in the bedroom is a night where you don't role-play.

8. Your laundry bills are higher than other couples' because you're constantly cleaning your sheets. That Gamora body paint really does get everywhere.

9. When you move in together you have a lot of big decisions to make—namely, what to do now that you have two box sets of *Firefly*.

10. You do not have to figure out what to do with your double gaming consoles, but you will need two TVs.

11. Choosing to get married feels like the biggest decision you'll ever make until you have to decide which nerdy theme you want for your wedding. You only get one chance to get married; will it be Hogwarts or Hobbiton?

12. Picking jewelry for the wedding isn't any easier. What will you wear forever? The One Ring of Power or a Green Lantern ring?

13. Forgiveness is important in every relationship, and especially when you kill each other in *Overwatch*.

14. Your idea of a romantic evening is a long walk together to catch Pokémon.

15. Your vacation involves taking the same week off work to play the new *Mass Effect*.

16. You agree on making extravagant, nerdy purchases to make your life more badass. You also agree on never taking them out of the boxes.

17. You have someone to support you emotionally every few years as you mourn the loss of the most recent Doctor.

18. People ask if you ever role-play in the bedroom and you're like, "Outside of the bedroom too!"

19. Decorating the walls becomes a nonissue since every available space is covered with shelves of toys, DVDs, or comic books. The upside of this is you've gained the superpower to assemble Ikea shelves like a pro.

20. Some days you talk more through Twitter than you do aloud.

21. You've got a drawer full of adapter cables. You don't need any of them but you will never clean it out. They are yours forever.

22. The most exciting part of your week is when you get to tell your significant other about a new superhero movie or casting announcement they haven't heard about yet.

23. If you have kids, you have to explain the difference between your toys and their toys.

24. You don't have movie nights, you have marathon nights.

25. Halloween isn't about choosing a couple costume, it's about choosing *which* couple costume out of the dozen you already have.

26. Children and pets are not just members of your family but useful costume accessories and vital to group cosplays.

27. Halloween becomes tame and forgettable after you spend a few comic cons together.

28. Decorating the walls is about deciding which *Star Wars* posters say the most about you both.

29. You only go out to a bar because they're having a trivia night.

30. You have an amazing yet complicated entertainment system to provide your TV with all streaming services possibly needed (legal and illegal). This is great for you, bad for guests who don't know how to watch anything.

31. Neither of you knows when the local sports teams are doing sporty things in the city and constantly get stuck in sport traffic.

32. You both know when a con is happening and laugh at the non-nerds when they're stuck in con traffic.

33. Doing joint laundry runs the risk of not being able to figure out whose Batman shirt is whose.

34. Your dream vacations list is limited to New Zealand's *Lord of the Rings* tour or San Diego Comic-Con.

35. Neither of you has any restraint when it comes to buying nerdy household items and your purchases spiral out of control. This will become apparent when a non-nerdy family member stops by and looks mortified at having to use a Batman toaster and a pizza cutter shaped like the *Enterprise.*

36. You finally have a real-life person to talk to about the plot of your latest fanfiction and ask if your characters are OOC or not.

37. Sometimes you experiment in the bedroom. Science experiments, that is! (You also have sex, but science is still dope!)

38. You rejoice when the power goes out because now it's officially board game night.

39. You both panic equally at non-nerdy social functions because oh god what do regular people even talk about?

40. Neither of you figures out what regular people talk about and you resort to asking every person at the event if they've seen the latest Marvel movie.

41. You both agree to leave the event early.

42. It feels amazing.

43. You get noise complaints every Sunday night because you can't stop screaming, "Oh shit!" during episodes of *The Walking Dead*.

44. You pioneer amazing new cuddle positions that accommodate phone reading, tablet playing, and console gaming at the same time.

45. You don't say, "I love you." You say, "I know."

46. You understood that reference.

47. Or you express your love in any of the following amazingly awful ways:

"I'm gonna call you Jean because you've been in my mind all day."

"You turn my blackest nights into my brightest days."

"You're an angel, but not a scary one from *Doctor Who*, or an asshole one from *Supernatural*, like, a classic angel."

"You're hotter than the Human Torch in summer."

"I want to spend all my extra lives with you."

"I would walk into Mordor for you."

"You're super, I'm just Saiyan."

"Will you be my dungeon master? Whips or dice, I'm cool with either."

"I ship us."

48. On special occasions you buy each other books instead of flowers.

49. You get to skip over the nerve-racking "showing each other your favorite movie or show" phase of the relationship because you've both for sure already seen it.

50. After a fight you ask each other if you can Ctrl+Alt+Delete because you'd like to restart.

ACE PILOT

BY DYLAN "NDR" EDWARDS

SOME OF MY EARLIEST MEMORIES ARE INEXTRICABLY LINKED TO A CERTAIN L. SKYWALKER:

POP

I GUESS THEY DON'T MAKE 'EM LIKE THEY USED TO.

4-year-old curmudgeon

POOR OL' LUKE.

NOT AS SEXY AS HAN.

NOT AS IMPOSING AS VADER.

B-B-BUT TOSCHE STATION!

POWER CONVERTERS!

KINDA WHINY.

EVEN SO, I ALWAYS HAD A SOFT SPOT FOR HIM. I NEVER QUITE GOT THE HATE.

CAN'T SAY I WAS ONE OF THOSE TRANS KIDS WHO *ALWAYS KNEW.*

BUT, WHILE I WAS ALWAYS VERY FOND OF LEIA...

(even went as her for Halloween once)

...LUKE WAS THE ONE I HAD MORE OF A SENSE OF WANTING TO *BE.*

HIS IMPULSIVENESS IS ALWAYS FOCUSED ON DOING WHAT IS GOOD AND WHAT IS RIGHT:

GET YOUR BUTT BACK HERE!

YOU GOT CLASSES STILL!

BRB, GOTTA DITCH SCHOOL TO SAVE MY FRIENDS.

MOVIE ROMANCES ALWAYS PUT ME OFF, FOR WHATEVER REASON.

=YAWN=

I'M NOT TOTALLY AROMANTIC, BUT I DO FIND IT DIFFICULT TO FEEL ANYTHING FOR THESE PAIRINGS.

A NEW HOPE INITIALLY TRIED TO FORCE LUKE INTO A STEREOTYPICAL STORY LINE:

YOU'RE THE YOUNG HERO, SO YOU GOTTA HAVE A ROMANCE WITH A PRINCESS.

THIS COULD GET AWKWARD.

I HAD MY OWN IMPOSED NARRATIVES:

YOU'RE A GIRL.

YOU'LL GET MARRIED.

YOU'LL HAVE KIDS.

THE 2000s, I FELL OUT OF LOVE WITH *STAR WARS*:

THE PREQUELS

OVERSATURATION

THESE SCENES ARE LIFTED DIRECTLY FROM *HIDDEN FORTRESS*!

BEING *THAT* NERD

HE FORCE AWAKENS DIDN'T DO IT FOR ME:

THESE SCENES ARE LIFTED DIRECTLY FROM *A NEW HOPE*!

BUT AFTER THE 2016 ELECTION, *ROGUE ONE* TURNED OUT TO BE SOMETHING I NEEDED:

CRUSH THE NAZIS!!

(I don't actually talk in the theater, I promise)

N A SEA OF MERCHANDISE THAT NOW FELT LIKE IT WAS GLORIFYING FASCISM, *SYMBOLS* OF LUKE'S SELF-SACRIFICING HEROISM TOOK ON A NEW MEANING.

Rebel Alliance logo

IN 2016, MARK HAMILL SAID THIS IN RESPONSE TO A QUESTION ABOUT LUKE'S SEXUAL ORIENTATION:

I'D SAY IT IS MEANT TO BE INTERPRETED BY THE VIEWER.

IF YOU THINK LUKE IS GAY, OF COURSE HE IS.

"YOU COULD THINK OF HIM THAT WAY IF YOU WANT" IS NOT AS POWERFUL A STATEMENT AS "HE DEFINITELY IS."

BUT LEAVING LUKE'S SEXUALITY UP FOR GRABS (SO TO SPEAK) DOES MEAN MY HEADCANON OF HIM AS ASEXUAL IS TOTES VALID, TOO.

MAYBE MY CONNECTION TO LUKE ISN'T A ROMANTIC FEELING, EXACTLY.

BUT IT'S AN ATTRACTION ALL THE SAME.

(Wedge was always n secret cutie crush)

©2017 D...NR

WE WILL NEVER BE BACK HERE AGAIN

Saadia Muzaffar

Reconnaissance

I've never really stopped thinking about that dream—the one in which I was stuck in a game where I was running from danger, and as I kept running forward trying to find a way out, the ground crumbled behind me so I could only move forward. In the unending time lapse of dreams, it felt like I had been running for days when somewhere, unbeknownst to me, the feeling morphed from dread to liberation. I woke up with a start, my heart pounding, and my mind struggling to name some profound realization I had just received but couldn't define.

Sometimes real life feels like a lucid dream. Like that time when I ended up on Tinder because I did not have the patience to sit through eHarmony's million questions, and got matched with someone who had just moved to Toronto from a small town in New Brunswick where Tinder's geolocation basically just laughed at you for trying.

Because Tinder only showed us the little blurb we wrote about ourselves, our ages, and our first names, there wasn't much to go by, except his blurb said he didn't want to have regrets on his deathbed (cheerful!) and mine said I was a feminist killjoy (got that out of the way early), and that geeky morosity felt almost comforting in a sea of curated, sunshiny profiles.

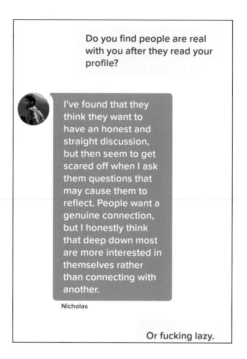

Do you find people are real with you after they read your profile?

I've found that they think they want to have an honest and straight discussion, but then seem to get scared off when I ask them questions that may cause them to reflect. People want a genuine connection, but I honestly think that deep down most are more interested in themselves rather than connecting with another.

Nicholas

Or fucking lazy.

Our first conversation was so unadorned and brazen and honest that it stunned us both by its radical simplicity. I didn't even say hello, because my guard was down from a long day, and a tired conversation at 11:00 p.m. at night yielded a clairvoyant impatience that should be a virtue. I listened intently, but as I typed my visceral replies, I wondered if he felt like I was going for the jugular; so intense and jaded, with a perfect stranger that I presumably wanted to like me.

As I fell asleep, I remember thinking, what would it be like to speak my mind to someone, unafraid? To not worry that they would misconstrue what I really meant? Is it courageous to explore that? Or is that reckless in a culture that favors curation of our personal brand every single mundane time we share something with the world? Could I just believe that they would trust the goodness in me as the default baseline for every word they heard? Last thoughts are the most lofty—with mine slipping into realizing that I had spent years reclaiming being myself but didn't know if it would be possible to be part of something like a twosome and still retain that.

Armistice

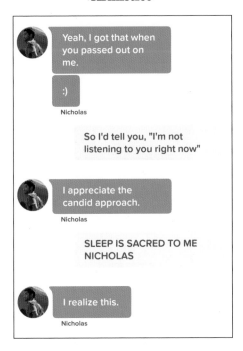

I found him good humored and not easily threatened by occasional inattention and plain truths. There was a weird otherworldly calm about him when he replied in lowercase after my ALL-UPPERCASE DECLARATIONS. Our conversations flowed naturally and felt easy and that terrified me. It's good that it feels "easy," right? That when I say what I mean he hears what I said? No more, no less? That I didn't have to hedge my words or my tone or my intentions? Is that what moving through the world should feel like for someone in my body? That unfamiliarity bore a hole into my protective mind moats and I found myself hyperaware of all of the ways I was *not* feeling.

Overwatch

Somewhere in that first week, we realized that we had talked a whole bunch without getting into the whole so-what-do-you-do-for-a-living shorthand. We still didn't know each other's last names, what schools we went to, or any other Google-identifiable details. Tinder could conk out on us tomorrow and we would have no way of finding each other.

> But one thing I've enjoyed so far is how little we know about each other.

> That sounds weird, but I like that I'm able to get to know you through your persona, and not through what you do, where you're from, etc.

> I feel like that other stuff is irrelevant, because I'm seeing a deeper side of you.

Nicholas

I was thinking that this evening too

This is in a weird kind of vacuum -off the grid

Even as I liked that he thought about things the way he did, reimagining convention with irreverence and hope—I found his nonhurry and tenderness disarming. My long-shored defenses against cloying poetics failed to raise flags when he said things like "deeper side of you," and the unfamiliarity of that safety felt less like relief and more like a reason to check if my battery light was off because the battery was fine or because the light had blown.

Coup de grâce

All this notwithstanding, we decided to see how long we could go without fessing up to any personal specifics. Our game-theory hearts established the rules as we waded into this marsh of what would in hindsight be social experimentation, but at that time just felt like the most obvious and fun way to move forward. We acknowledged that in staying anonymous, it would mean we couldn't fall on the shorthand of coded commerce or social hierarchy or family background to define who we were. We could talk about what places meant to us, but not by their names. It meant we had to trust what the other person was conveying about how something or someplace *felt to them* and let that be truth enough. Our conversations became gentle daily unravelings of things we had learnt, what had caught us when we fell, and who had helped us soar.

In the past few years I found myself quite isolated due to where I was living. Being around friends has allowed me to come out of myself again. That's what amazing people bring to your life, acceptance of who you are on multiple levels. I know what you mean when you speak of being around people you're grateful to call friends.

You'll probably be asleep by the time I get back. I just arrived in the city with some friends, we left late from the cottage. I'm pretty wrecked, but will write before bed.

Escalade

I remember thinking in hindsight how we skirted all notions of noblesse or higher moral ground. It became a game. A fun but deeply committed game. A secret language. A discipline. Our promise to do this was really for the adventure of it but also because it challenged us to reimagine what a journey to finding who the other person is could become if we broke all the rules.

What followed were hundreds of exchanges that ended up being a version of what my dad did when he wanted to let my mum know that he was seriously into her. He wrote her a very long letter detailing his strengths and his weaknesses, his fears and ambitions, and what kind of life he wanted to build with his partner. He said he wanted her to have a full picture of what it was that he was asking her to consider, and that he knew that if she took a chance on his hustling entrepreneur and engineer butt, it would mean a Not Always Smooth Ride™ but it would always be full of adventure.

This was in the seventies. She said yes.

So the fact that forty years later, my exchanges ended up mirroring that forthrightness is both charming and scary. Is this how cycles get created? Both good and bad?

Dust-off

I flailed in the downside of being completely honest and whether I would scare someone away by being too much—a thing I've known and been reminded of since I was a little girl. Too smart, too curious, too bold, too mouthy, too spirited, too quick, too sure. But the upside, if it didn't deter him, would be that he would get to know me in a way only I knew me. I found myself wondering if that would actually feel good, being so vulnerable. Would I feel lighter in my steps? Or is truth heavier to carry? Would I feel like I was code-switching between him and the world all the time if he really saw me? Is that a bad thing? It dawned on me that I didn't really know what that is actually like. But I had a cape in this untraceable anonymity. I was on this quest. It was worth the risk.

Tête-de-pont

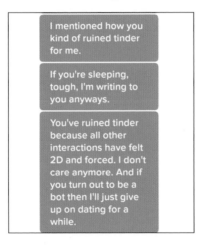

I mentioned how you kind of ruined tinder for me.

If you're sleeping, tough, I'm writing to you anyways.

You've ruined tinder because all other interactions have felt 2D and forced. I don't care anymore. And if you turn out to be a bot then I'll just give up on dating for a while.

I found that I was waiting to exhale as I read what he wrote and how achingly honest it felt to hear him acknowledge the emotional labor of dating. I caught myself thinking that I liked him, immediately followed by a frenzy of reasons why it was too soon to be saying this to myself about a person who I didn't "know" anything about. Again, my defenses failed to raise flags—that unfamiliarity was beginning to feel really familiar—so I settled into accepting that it probably was too early, whatever that meant, but just this once, I wanted to give myself permission to feel this glorious warmth, and if it ended up burning me, so be it.

Surrender

We met three times during those six weeks of anonymity. Yes, yes, you can continue being anonymous even in the real world. It happens in movies all the time. It made us do silly things like separating our kayaks mid-whitewater so one of us could take a call from our family, and serious things like being quiet in each other's company as we paddled downriver on a sunny day and marveled at the cicadas calling, and that mattered more than anything else we could have said or validated in that moment.

We set a date for the big reveal. It felt like the end of a beginning. It felt bittersweet after weeks of just being. Sharing stories that sounded like they could've been from anywhere, except they were ours. There was no name-dropping; there was a lot of what-did-you-mean-when-you-saids and how-did-that-make-you-feels. A lot of talk of darkness and being broken and imperfect because there was nothing particularly shiny to hide behind. We were flotsam in a sea of voluntary anonymity, very aware of the precariousness of this very real, very solid connection we had found in each other.

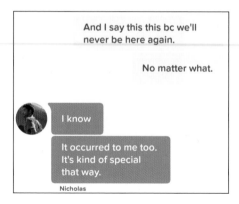

I felt *hiraeth* slowly soaking through my skin: grief, some deep sadness for a home that never was. I felt grateful and confused and surefooted, all at the same time. It was bizarrely liberating to only be excited about learning more but not really caring because all this other data felt like gravy.

I thought of that dream again, the one where I was running from danger in a game and had the ground crumble behind me as I ran, so I couldn't go back. I thought about how much these six weeks felt like only being able to move forward because it almost didn't matter where I had already been, except I had gotten what I needed from it. A singular mode of forward thrust into the unknown that lay ahead.

I felt a warm feeling course through my veins as I figured out why the dread had morphed into an effervescent liberation—it was because wherever I'd been, whatever I had done, mattered as much or as little as I wanted it to, because I would never be back there again. I was free to move forward and be as much or as little of anything in this tiny little sanctuary we had started to shape.

I took a deep breath, clasping my Google-at-the-ready phone with one hand and squeezing his palm with the other. I told him about this dream that has followed me for years as I found his kind and reciprocally apprehensive gaze, both of us bracing to feel the ground behind us already starting to crumble.

"My last name is Muzaffar. Who are you out there?"

GENDERQUEER

BY MAIA KOBABE

BIAS

AT THE QUEER COMICS EXPO IN S.F. I SAW AN ARTIST WHO I JUST TABLED NEAR AT VANCAF.

These are great!

Thank you!

If I had known you were gay I would have stopped to read your books much earlier!

※1

MISTAKE

Tyler Cohen, bisexual comics author and mom

So, what does your husband do?

Umm— I don't call him my husband...

I prefer "partner," it's less gender binary...

Of course! Sorry!

LATER

I should be better at this...

※44

SECRETS

ONE OF MY FIRST CLASSES AT CCA WAS AUTOBIOGRAPHY COMICS TAUGHT BY MARINAOMI.

A good way to get started is by listing your biggest secrets — at least one of them should suggest a story!

NOPE

No one gets my secrets. They are MINE!

※45

CENSORED

I did write a short comic about one of my "gender demons" in that class but I was so embarrassed by it that I taped pieces of paper over those two pages of my sketchbook.

※47

DREAM KING

N HIGH SCHOOL I READ NEIL GAIMAN'S "SANDMAN" FOR THE FIRST TIME.

One night I decided to ask Morpheus to send me a good dream...

I then dreamed about having a massive painful boner that lasted all day.

IN THE MORNING

Huh

#23

SENSATION

MY HETERO-FLEXIBLE FRIEND TRYING TO EXPLAIN WHY SHE LIKES LESBIAN PORN MORE THAN GAY PORN.

I don't know how to assign a sensation to a body part that I don't have

I assign sensation to a body part I don't have *all the time.* Sometimes I can almost feel where it would be

resting against my thigh

#32

REALIZATION

I remember when I first realized I never had to have children.

It was like walking out of a narrow alley

into a wide-open field.

#59

GIFTS

I never have to get married

I never have to date anyone

I don't even have to care about sex

THESE REALIZATIONS WERE LIKE GIFTS THAT I GAVE TO MYSELF.

#60

MK
2017

COSPLAY

Hope Larson

"I'm only in town for the weekend. Do you want to meet up?"

I was in the tub, on Tinder, the night before a show. You know—a convention. Comic books. People wearing inflatable T. rex costumes. A miasma of BO and Sharpies. I was in town a little ahead of my friends, and I'd just handed in a script. I was standing at the point furthest from my last deadline, before starting my orbit back toward the next one. It's the only time I feel truly relaxed, and I was determined not to blow the moment alone in my hotel room.

I was seeing someone, but it was early in our not-technically-a-relationship. We were both playing it very cool and I didn't know if there was "anything there." I was almost hoping there wouldn't be, because I was considering leaving Los Angeles in the spring. It was definitely too early to send neurotic, girlfriend-y texts from the hotel room my publisher had paid for. So: enter Tinder.

The selection was nothing like LA's parade of aspiring actors and dark-spectacled comedy writers. Here they mostly worked in tech, and looked too conservative for me, or oozed financial security in a way that I found off-putting.

Gene, with his floppy Oasis hair and stylish jacket, stood out among them. We matched; we chatted. He didn't seem like a serial killer.

"Do you want to meet up? Like, now?"

Sometimes loneliness makes me bold.

He suggested a bar which happened to be a short walk from my hotel, not that I was about to tell him where I was staying. I got there early, like I always do, to buy my own drink and avoid the dance over the check. I call this move the Conflict-Averse Feminist. I moved around the bar trying out different seating options, like one of Goldilocks's bears, until I located a spot that would allow for close conversation but didn't invite too much coziness.

When Gene showed up, he was cuter and taller than I thought he'd be, and talking to him was easy. He wasn't a comics guy, thank God, but he was still impressed that I wrote them for a living. (If you're a woman, writing comic books is like having a first-date superpower: it sends plenty of guys back in time to when they last read comics, as kids, and renders them easily defeated.)

I trotted out my best material: my most charming stories, my greatest hits. There was no rationing it out, or worrying that I'd built myself up to a sum greater than my parts. I'm not the type to dress up like Wonder Woman and trot around conventions, slipping into character for every amateur photographer, but I understand the impulse. This was my own brand of cosplay, and I was in disguise as myself. I wanted to be seen, and yet remain unknown. I wanted to appear at the ball like Cinderella, and vanish at midnight back to the shabby garret from whence I came. My costume was tinfoil and papier-mâché, but it was convincing enough for an evening—and not just for him. I was dressing up for myself, too. It had been a hard few years, and the shame of the mess I'd gotten into was intense. Tonight, I was indulging in a fantasy where that shame did not exist, because there was no future where I would have to confront it.

As for Gene, his company was the perfect vaccination for my immediate stressor, a long weekend of self-promotion. Before tonight, he'd never heard my name, or read my Wikipedia page, or seen *that* movie. He wasn't asking me to soft pitch the plot of my comic book, or give his fifteen-year-old nephew tips on breaking in. Like me, he was grateful just for the company.

We finished our drinks. I didn't want to keep drinking, but I still wasn't sure what I wanted from him. I wasn't sure if the night would end in somebody's bed, but I knew it wasn't going to end in mine, because I had a hotel roommate. Gene offered to drive me around and show me the local sites, as much as you can show them at ten p.m., and that sounded perfect to me.

We went outside to his car, and I buckled up before leaning over and kissing him. He was a great kisser.

He started the car. While he tried to work out where we were headed, he skipped through the CD in the player, and finally ejected it.

"Open the glove box," he said.

Inside were stacks of burned CDs in little plastic sleeves, each one labeled with a year. 1983, 1990, 2005 . . .

"What is this?" I asked.

He explained: Last year, he'd moved away and taken a job in a shitty Midwestern town. He didn't know anyone, and he'd spent a lonely Independence Day weekend composing a mix of songs from every year he'd been alive. It was, to me, a profoundly charming detail of the version of him I was constructing in my head, like a character in one of my stories.

"Pick one," he said.

I pulled something from the early nineties, which seemed appropriate, considering his Britpop hair.

"When you're a kid," I said, "the movies tell you this is what it'll be like when you're a teenager. Driving around at night with cute guys, talking. Is it like that for anyone? It definitely wasn't for me."

"Me either."

The whole night was beginning to feel unreal, a thirty-something mash-up of *American Graffiti* and *Before Sunrise*. An unfamiliar city, a charming boy, a girl passing through, and a killer soundtrack. We parked outside a second bar and stared at the entrance, but never got out of the car. Instead, we went back to his place.

He lived in a microefficiency apartment in a brand-new building that looked nice from the outside. His apartment was so small that he had to lean the bed against the wall during the day, and it didn't have a private kitchen. The developers had saved space by opting for a communal one downstairs. And there was no door on the bathroom—not even a curtain. I couldn't stop laughing about that. Was the housing crisis so bad here that *doors* had become a luxury item?

He protested that the place was temporary; he'd rented it sight unseen, desperate to get away from the shitty Midwestern town and the lonely summer of mix CDs. I told him about my own living situation, which wasn't so different: two roommates, a combination bedroom and office, a twin bed crammed into an alcove next to the bookshelf. God help me if there were ever an earthquake. The movies had been even less honest about our thirties than they had about our teens.

But they weren't wrong about everything. Gene and I had the sort of chemistry you see ten feet tall on a movie screen. Under its influence, time moved differently, like the DP was cranking the camera too fast, dropping frames to better thrill the audience. We had gone through the looking glass and through the wardrobe. We were on an unfamiliar planet where the usual questions did not apply: Do you want kids? Do you want to get married? What's your game plan? Do you have any debt?

Who cares, when three blue moons are rising and gravity's so weak that you can fly?

I hadn't expected this, when we were sitting in the bar, but he had.

"When I walked in and saw you," he said, "it was like all the lights in the room went out, and you were all I could see."

It was, and is, the most romantic thing a man has ever said to me.

I had obligations in the morning, and I had to get back to my hotel, but I wanted to see him again. Did he want to? Would it be all right, even with the clock ticking in the background?

"I'm not going to break your heart, am I? When I leave?"

"Well," he said, "I mean, you definitely are."

Regardless, we made plans to meet again. Maybe that's why flings are called flings: because you throw yourself into them, and to hell with the consequences.

♥

My convention schedule was a minefield of signings, business dinners, panels, and press. I went from meetings with my intimidating Big Two bosses, to putting on my public face for fans, to catching up with old friends. It was exhausting to play so many roles for so many people. I wasn't sleeping much, and the stress/caffeine/alcohol were hell on my skin. When I wasn't on the con floor, I walked around the city, headphones on, and hunted for records on which to blow my per diem.

What would it be like if I lived here? Would Gene and I be a couple? Would that work? If I took him back to the real world, my world, would he survive? I was barely surviving Los Angeles myself. He was a sweet boy, and I had a cart full of baggage. I'd left it on the tarmac at the airport, but it would be back on my doorstep when I got home, and I'd have to change out of my shiny disguise and put on my thrift-store rags.

♥

The next time I saw Gene, I was in costume literally as well as metaphorically. I was coming from a party with a dress code that asked, "If you were a god, what would you look like?"

I'd packed my eyelids with black eye shadow and glitter, slithered into high-waisted jeans, and pushed glow-stick bracelets onto my arms. I was probably wearing my signature motorcycle jacket, an acid-washed denim version from the eighties that I'd scored off Etsy. Purchased in an attempt to look tough while hanging out at the club where my DJ ex worked and discourage creeps from hitting on me, it had turned out to have the opposite effect and functioned as a conversation piece. But I loved it anyway.

Gene pulled up at the curb outside the party, and I jumped into his car.

To spare us (or spare him) his hated apartment, he'd booked a hotel room, and as we walked in, I caught a smirk from the man at the desk. I was suddenly aware that my low-key goddess getup read very differently late at night in a hotel than it did at a party full of nerds. We looked like a prostitute and her john, or maybe a long-term couple playing dress-up, fumbling after their lost spark. I laughed it off. The desk clerk could see what he wanted to see.

But I worried about Gene. Had I put one over on him? I hadn't meant to. I hadn't known this one-in-a-million connection would complicate things. For me, it ultimately changed nothing: when the week ended, we'd say goodbye, and I'd go home.

One look at his face, and I knew it was different for him.

My last day of the show was a short one. I didn't have many commitments, and when they wrapped, Gene and I drove out to the beach.

It was unseasonably warm, and we lay on the sand, soaking up the rays of Earth's yellow sun, talking.

He offered to go back with me. To LA. To set his whole life aside and step into mine. I was touched by the offer, but I'd been in his shoes, and I knew that no matter how earnestly it was offered, this was a gift too precious for me to accept.

"You can't do that," I said. "I can't ask you to do that."

"You're not asking me to."

"I know. But you can't. Please don't."

"But we should keep in touch. We can talk on the phone. Remember phones? We can stay friends. You never know."

We did talk, once, but I cut the friendship off not long after. I didn't want to give him any more false hope than I already had. Sometimes breaking the boy's heart is the right thing to do.

Ending it was unquestionably my responsibility, but I hated that I had to. Hadn't I been clear? I'd told him at the start that this was just a weekend. Why hadn't he taken me at my word? Why had he tried to change the rules of the game? Why couldn't we have had a nice time and then called it a day, like adults?

"Men don't listen," said my ex. "We hear what we want to hear."

But if Gene was fooling himself, maybe I was, too. I'd put too much stock in my performance, but was I really controlling things as much as

I thought? He'd put on an act, too, with his haircut and his glove box of CDs, and I'd taken the bait. And the chemistry between us was an element of chaos that neither of us could override.

"When I walked in and saw you, it was like all the lights in the room went out, and you were all I could see."

I will never forget that weekend. There isn't a moment I regret. Even though it wasn't meant to last, it was an experience that uncovered depths of human experience (or, at least, human biology) that I didn't know existed, or didn't believe were real.

In the end, I did leave LA, and went back to Asheville, where I grew up. Despite my reservations, the place fits like a glove. It should—it's small enough. Like my friend T says, "This town is the size of a dime."

I'm no longer ashamed of who I am, or where my journey has taken me, because in the end, this is where I'm meant to be. I'm happy. I don't need a costume anymore—luckily, because in a small town we all know each other's secrets, so what good would that do? I have nothing to prove, nothing to hide. I don't know where I'm going, but I know where I'll be next year. And when I meet another boy who lights up the night and slows down time, I won't have to keep him at arm's length. My life has a space for him, now, and I'm ready to let him in.

WIFE
HANNA-PIRITA LEHKONEN

WHEN I MET MY WIFE, I MET A CUTE TOMBOY GIRL.

WHEN I MARRIED MY WIFE, I MARRIED THE MOST FEMININE WOMAN I KNEW.

WHEN I CELEBRATED OUR THIRD ANNIVERSARY WITH MY WIFE, I CELEBRATED IT WITH A TRANS MAN.

AND NOW I'M WAITING FOR OUR SEVEN-YEAR ANNIVERSARY WITH AN AGENDER PERSON.

ALL THESE YEARS THEY HAVE WANTED ME TO AVOID ALL GENDERED WORDS AND PRONOUNS.

EXCEPT ONE...

WIFE

BECAUSE THEY ARE MY WIFE AND I AM THEIR HUSBAND.

AND I LOVE THEM NO MATTER HOW FLUID THEIR GENDER IS...

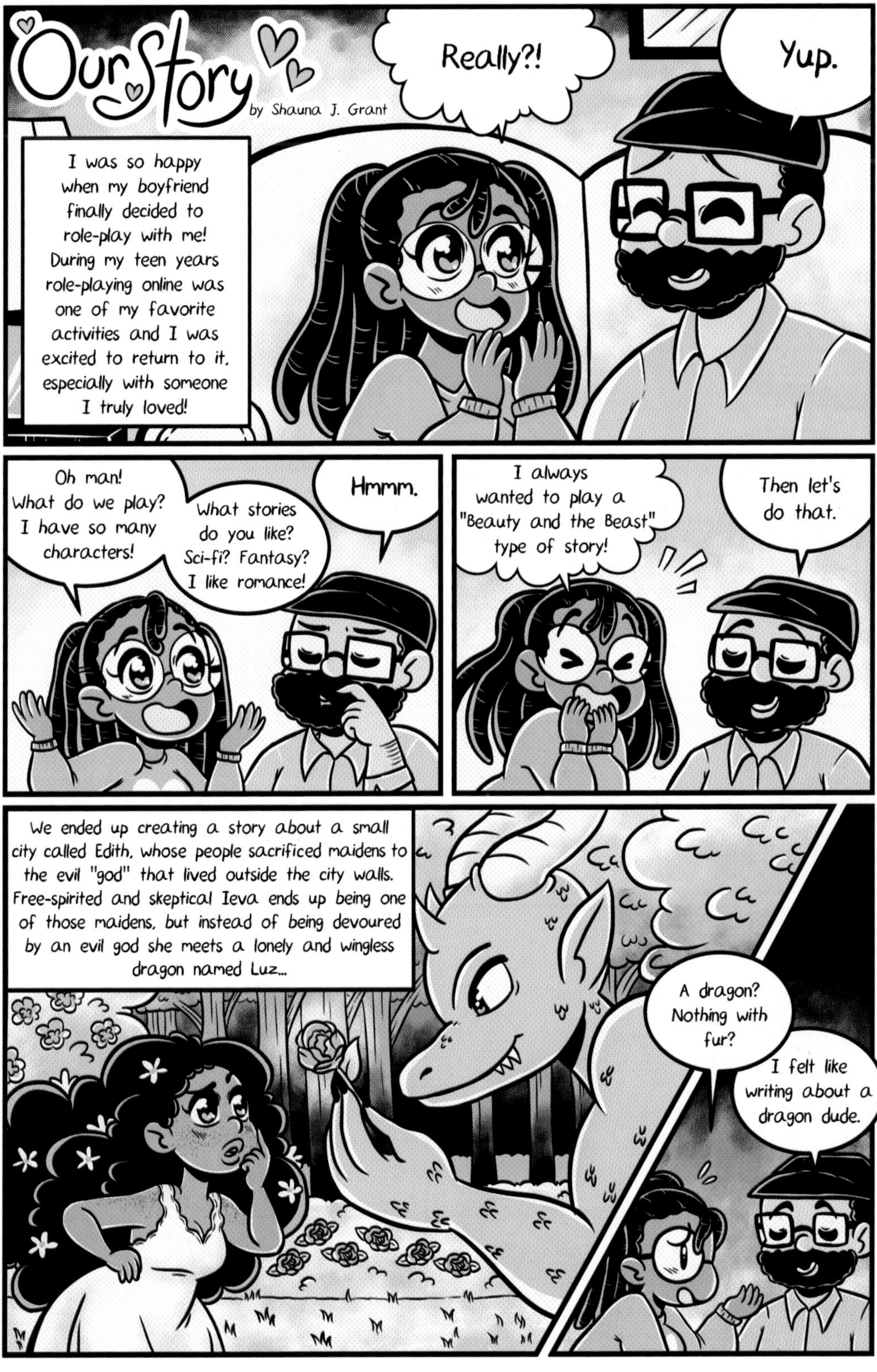

Our Story
by Shauna J. Grant
I was so happy when my boyfriend finally decided to role-play with me! During my teen years role-playing online was one of my favorite activities and I was excited to return to it, especially with someone I truly loved!
Really?!
Yup.
Oh man! What do we play? I have so many characters!
What stories do you like? Sci-fi? Fantasy? I like romance!
Hmmm.
I always wanted to play a "Beauty and the Beast" type of story!
Then let's do that.
We ended up creating a story about a small city called Edith, whose people sacrificed maidens to the evil "god" that lived outside the city walls. Free-spirited and skeptical Ieva ends up being one of those maidens, but instead of being devoured by an evil god she meets a lonely and wingless dragon named Luz...
A dragon? Nothing with fur?
I felt like writing about a dragon dude.

It was fun watching our characters grow as our story evolved from a simple romance to a story that explored the thirst for knowledge and themes of faith, obsession, and corrupted power.

Girl!

Heh

It was a big change from all the role-plays based on "Sonic" and "Yu-Gi-Oh!" in my teen years.

You have no idea what you're in store for in ten years!

Hey!

Me Age 16

I quickly fell in love with our story. My boyfriend was a passionate poet and his prose was filled with that same love...

...I was excited thinking of new ideas to share with him, creating illustrations of our characters, and spotting similarities of ourselves and our relationship in our stories.

As Luz and Ieva fought for their happily-ever-after...

...I thought about ours, too.

And during those times where we couldn't be together...

...Role-playing our story made him feel all the more close to me.

So I've been thinking...

Eventually our story had to end.

This was new to me. I never ended a role-play before—
the adventures just went on until they quietly fizzled out.

But WHY does it have to end...

Because all stories come to an end... It'll be a good one.

BUT I LOVE THEM...

WAAAH...

It's okay!

There will be more stories to love just as much!

Luz was no longer thought to be an evil god by the people of Edith. Ieva finally believed in love... And my boyfriend and I?

We got to feel what it was like to finally merge our creative worlds together.

...There are the stars that trail across your palm...

And he was right... There were more stories to love... Especially ours.

PROS AT CONS

(A Story in Prose of Consensual Sex)

Hope Nicholson

We've all done it. Or at least, a good number of us who are sexual and single—and a disappointing number of us who are not single—have. Con sex.

It's really unavoidable. Most of us are freelancers and work fairly alone. Our weird hours and erratic travel schedule (either holed up in our office or on the road for weeks) can make relationships difficult to create and maintain. Most creative professionals have leftover social anxiety from high school and childhood that still makes them shy and reluctant to try new things (like dating with strangers). And every summer we are thrown into this heady mix of praise, ego stroking, and money exchanges, with hundreds of thousands of new humans crowding us each day, and dozens of our respected (and rarely met-in-the-flesh peers) drinking to excess each night. It's a combo where if you are someone who likes touch and likes meeting new people, it would be almost impossible not to, at least once, smooch on someone.

And you can't talk about it, because despite all this, you are still there for business. This mix of personal and professional validation means any sex attached to any of it, natural and logical as it may seem, is heavily frowned upon. Those that violate the rules ("Do but don't speak of it," "Make arrangements so no one sees you") are whispered about after. Go back to their hotel room, sure, but don't do anything in the bar. Gossip reproduces perpetually, like cells in a lab, with people's romantic pasts dating back to the 1960s whispered about. People don't forget. And don't you want to be known for your work rather than who you spent a night with?

And yet, there you are. Drink in hand. Excitement bubbling to the surface. You're in a group of people. A colorist, an editor, a letterer, a cartoonist. People who get who you are and what you do. People who are, remarkably, very, very cute. It could be they are no cuter than people who pass you on the street all day, but here you are, and here they are, and is this person talking more to you than to other people? What title were they doing again? Quick, ask about it. No, wait, maybe it was canceled, don't ask about it! Ask about their dog! Shit, they probably have a cat. Most artists have cats. Oh, how do you signal you're interested in the clearest way possible?! Buy them a drink! Maybe they'll like you more if they're drunk too.

And how do you describe that tension of flirting, that feeling of "I think . . . I hope" that comes when you feel sparks fly? What is it that signals interest? Is it a gaze held too long? Is it a smile that is a bit wider? And even if there are sparks, a good deal of people enjoy the rush of chemistry and attraction without wanting to proceed further. And even if there is, and they want, you don't know if they're a good person.

And who has time to have panic attacks for the next two years or more if they're not, and have to face them in this same bar next summer, over and over again, like a sexual-misconduct version of *Groundhog Day*?

But have you ever tried to walk away from a flirtation? It's good advice to do so, maybe. But it's like telling someone to walk away from a dragon's hoard of gold. It's so rare, so unusual, and so completely overwhelming to feel that attention on you, to feel those warmth-giving hormones flood your brain and your body. It feels like an intrinsic good. Natural, and normal, and right. Yes, you could choose not to proceed. But also, no, you can't.

So, we've established that professionally, sex with colleagues is bad. Personally, it is a roll of the dice whether it will negatively affect you. And yet, cartoonists marry each other, editors marry artists, long-term relationships are built and nurtured, and it's all started through this moment of gazes at the bar. Why is it only considered acceptable to talk about once commitment is involved? How many months of texts and selfies and hookups in different cities until it's considered a commitment?

I'm making this all seem rather logical, aren't I? Reassuring you that you're not doing anything wrong? That sex by its nature should be free of consequences since it feels so good?

Well, no.

Sex is a fire. It can warm, it can destroy, it needs to be respected. You can't predict anyone's reactions. You can't predict your own reactions, even if you really are pretty sure you can (you can't). Check in, ask questions. Be a friend. Or at least, be a good human. You might not be able to control the fire, but you can control what you do after.

The pros of con sex, the cons of pro sex, are difficult to navigate. Good luck.

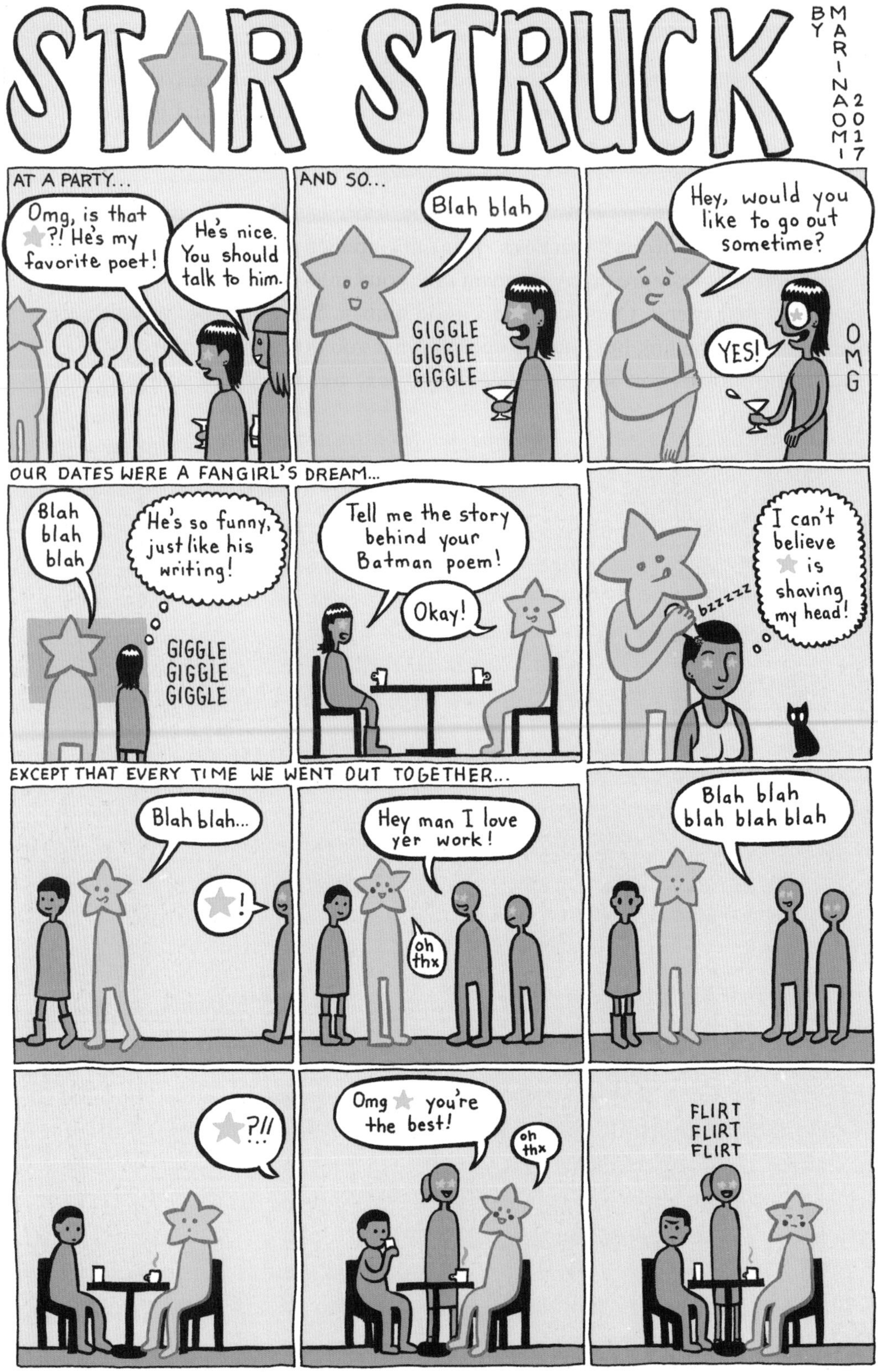
STAR STRUCK
BY MARINAOMI 2017
AT A PARTY...
Omg, is that ?! He's my favorite poet!
He's nice. You should talk to him.
AND SO...
Blah blah
GIGGLE GIGGLE GIGGLE
Hey, would you like to go out sometime?
YES!
OMG
OUR DATES WERE A FANGIRL'S DREAM...
Blah blah blah
He's so funny, just like his writing!
GIGGLE GIGGLE GIGGLE
Tell me the story behind your Batman poem!
Okay!
bzzzzz
I can't believe is shaving my head!
EXCEPT THAT EVERY TIME WE WENT OUT TOGETHER...
Blah blah...
!
Hey man I love yer work!
oh thx
Blah blah blah blah blah
?!! ...
Omg you're the best!
oh thx
FLIRT FLIRT FLIRT

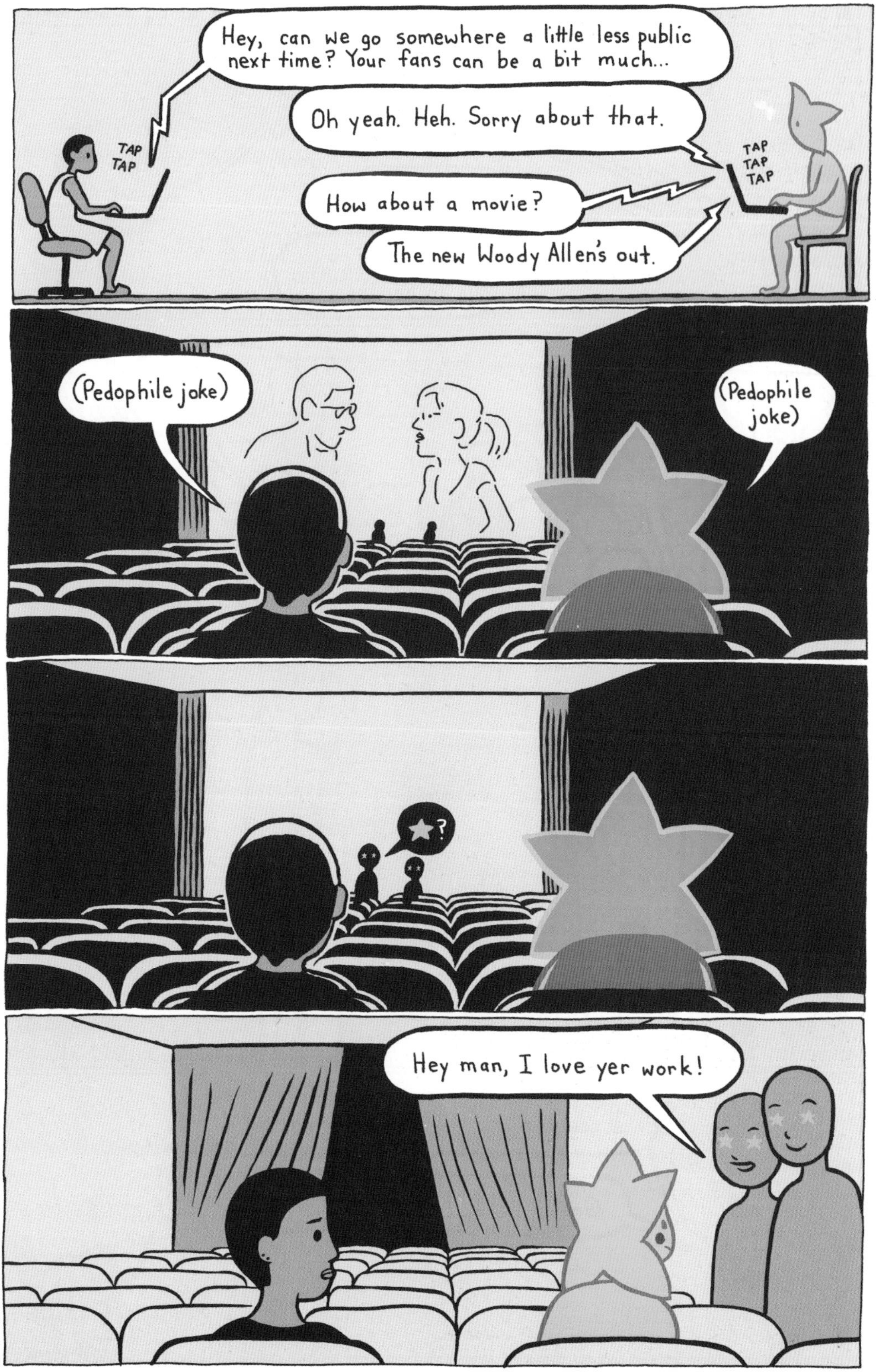
Hey, can we go somewhere a little less public next time? Your fans can be a bit much...
TAP TAP
Oh yeah. Heh. Sorry about that.
TAP TAP TAP
How about a movie?
The new Woody Allen's out.
(Pedophile joke)
(Pedophile joke)
?
Hey man, I love yer work!

WE DIDN'T DATE FOR LONG BUT WE STAYED FRIENDLY (AND I'M STILL A BIG FAN).

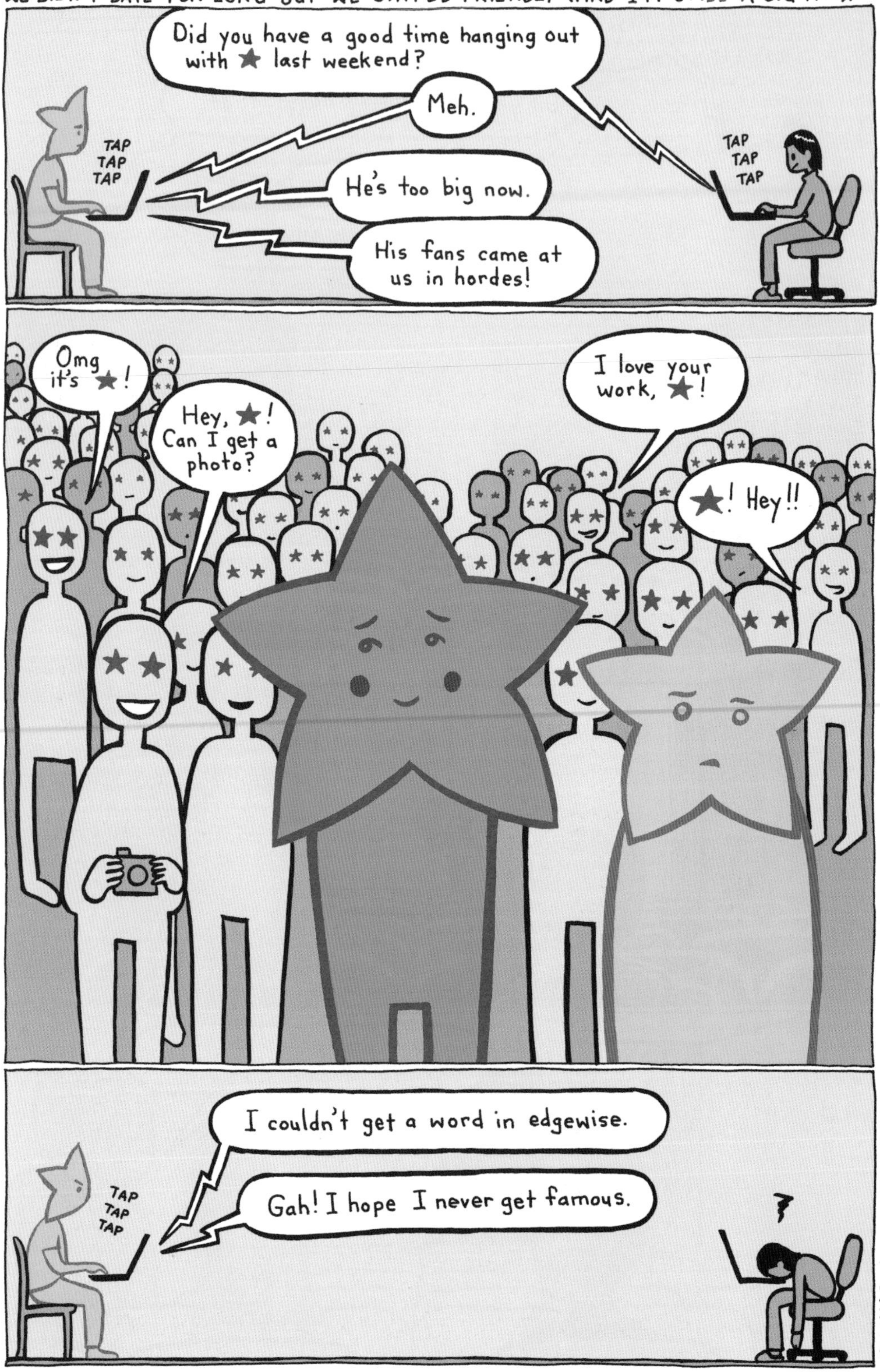

Did you have a good time hanging out with ★ last weekend?
TAP TAP TAP
TAP TAP TAP
Meh.
He's too big now.
His fans came at us in hordes!
Omg it's ★!
Hey, ★! Can I get a photo?
I love your work, ★!
★! Hey!!
I couldn't get a word in edgewise.
Gah! I hope I never get famous.
TAP TAP TAP

I tried to make an account on a popular fanfiction hosting site for this project, a way of making a tangible page out of my bad decisions and messy past, but it stopped me. Not only was I only permitted to upload a few at a time, there were a lot of hoops to jump through, to make sure I wasn't putting too much out there all at once.

Where the hell was that when I was 16? In my fanfiction, and my life?

Boy, this got me to thinking. Back in my day, the Wild West of the internet, there were no such limitations. From spam filters to hearts broken, there was nothing really there to hold us back from vomiting our entire hearts onto the page.

Recently, I compared my work to an owl pellet. (Those, I didn't mind dissecting in class, but the frog wasn't happening. At my core, I'm a softhearted Louis, not a bloodthirsty Lestat.) If you've ever taken apart an owl pellet, it's full of skeletons.

It's what the owl coughs up that it can't digest--feathers, bones, etc., but dissecting them can tell you a lot about where an owl's been, what it consumes.

Fanfiction, as a young woman, and my professional work now--

that's my owl pellet.

I hope that people dissect it, love it, take it apart, and swallow bits to include in their own owl pellets. I hope that if you take it apart and lay the pieces down, you can see what I consumed. The skeletons of vampires, of anime girls, of moody music and "five times I made out with a girl at a slumber party, and one time I didn't."

Tag my past for the warnings--
the infidelity,
the violence,
the mental illness, the mistakes.

I can't undo it, but I can tag for warnings. **(Tini Howard, 2017)**

"THEM STRUGGLES" - CHRISTINA "PEACHES" CORTES

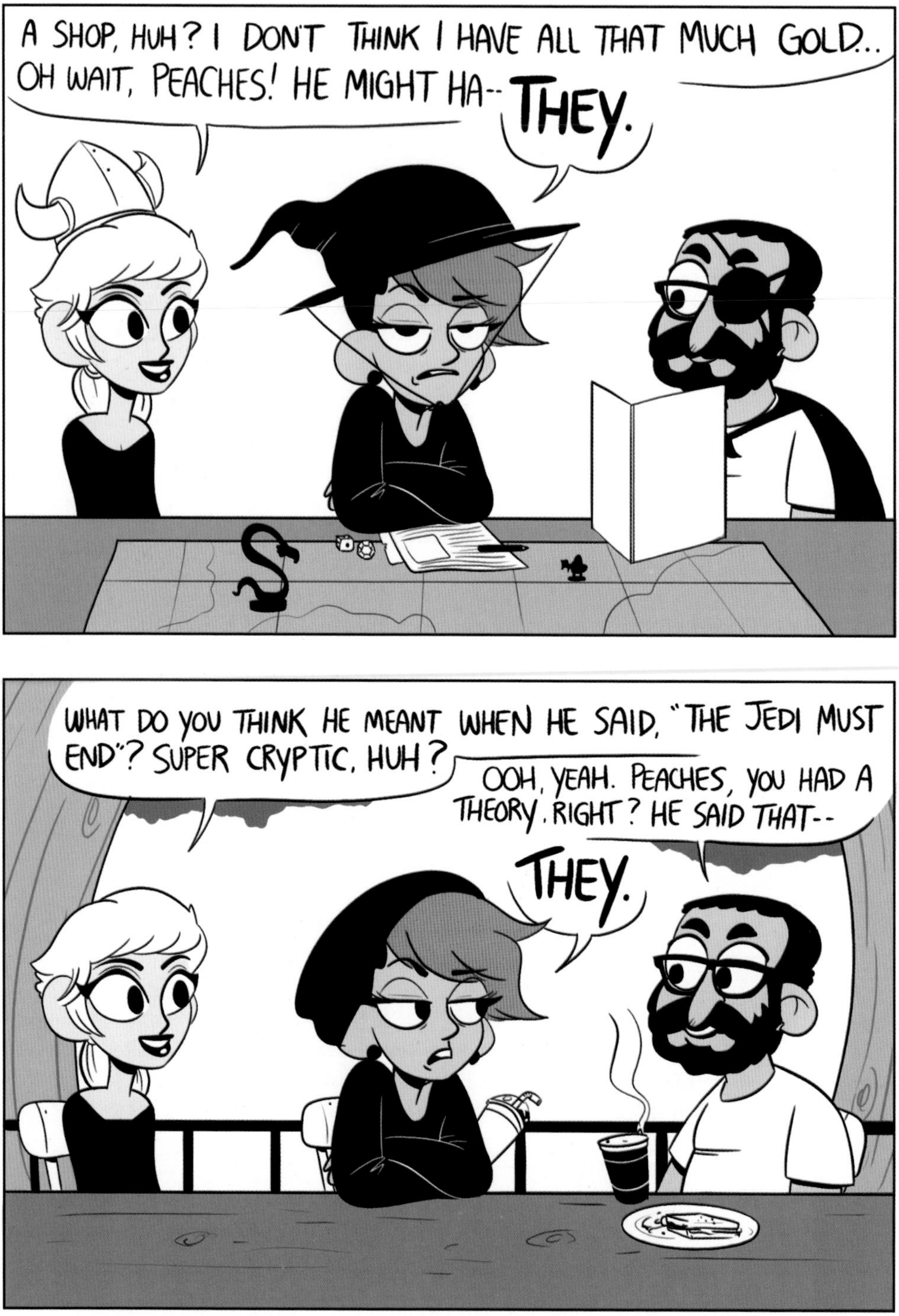
A SHOP, HUH? I DON'T THINK I HAVE ALL THAT MUCH GOLD.. OH WAIT, PEACHES! HE MIGHT HA--
THEY.
WHAT DO YOU THINK HE MEANT WHEN HE SAID, "THE JEDI MUST END"? SUPER CRYPTIC, HUH?
OOH, YEAH. PEACHES, YOU HAD A THEORY, RIGHT? HE SAID THAT--
THEY.

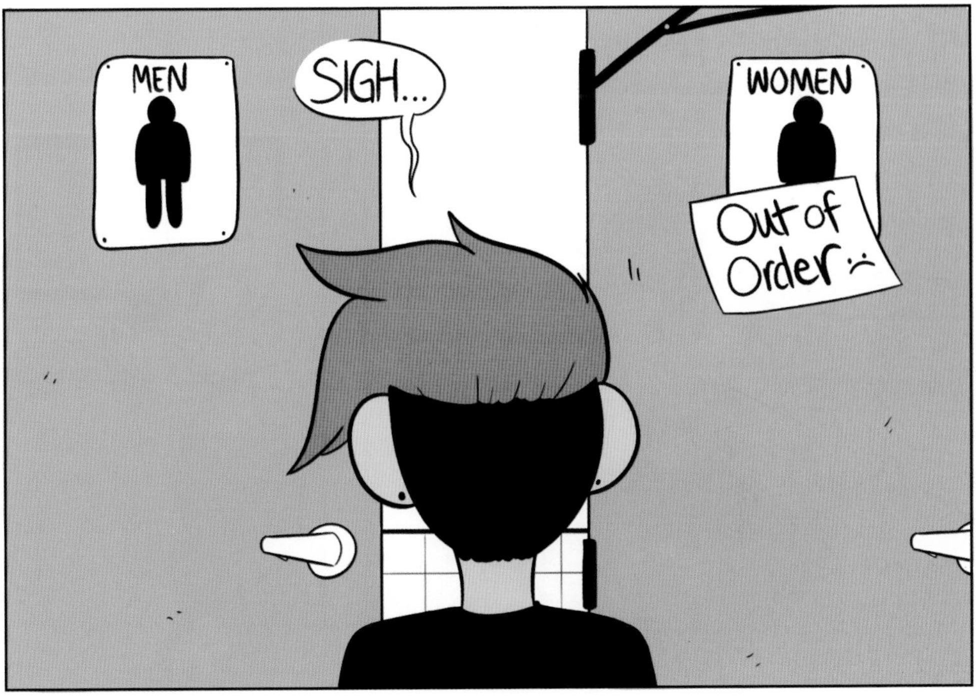
MEN
SIGH...
WOMEN
Out of Order

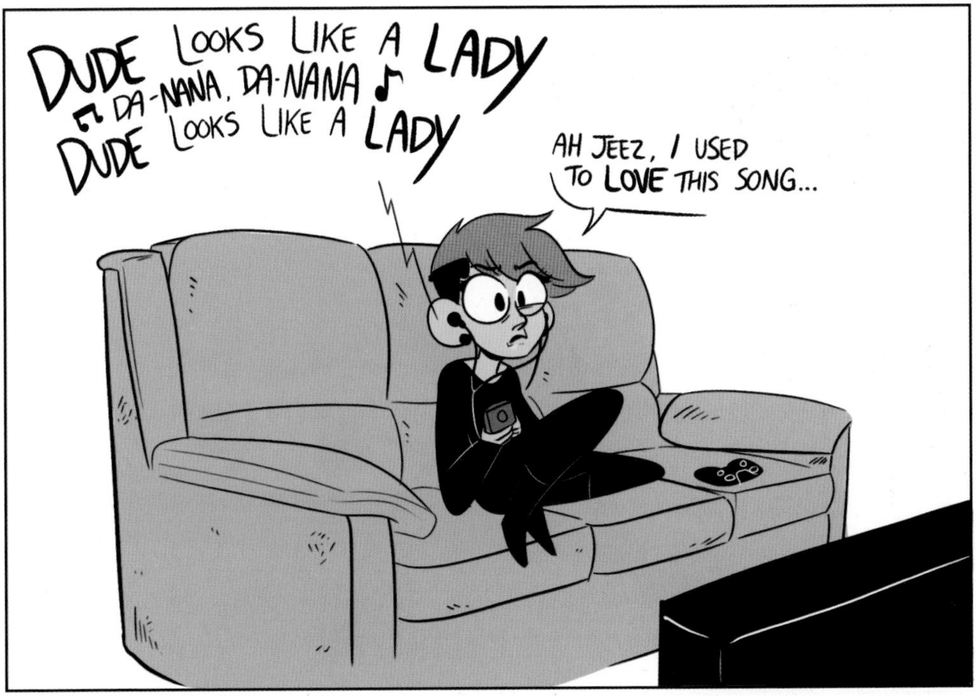
DUDE LOOKS LIKE A LADY
DA-NANA, DA-NANA
DUDE LOOKS LIKE A LADY
AH JEEZ, I USED TO LOVE THIS SONG...

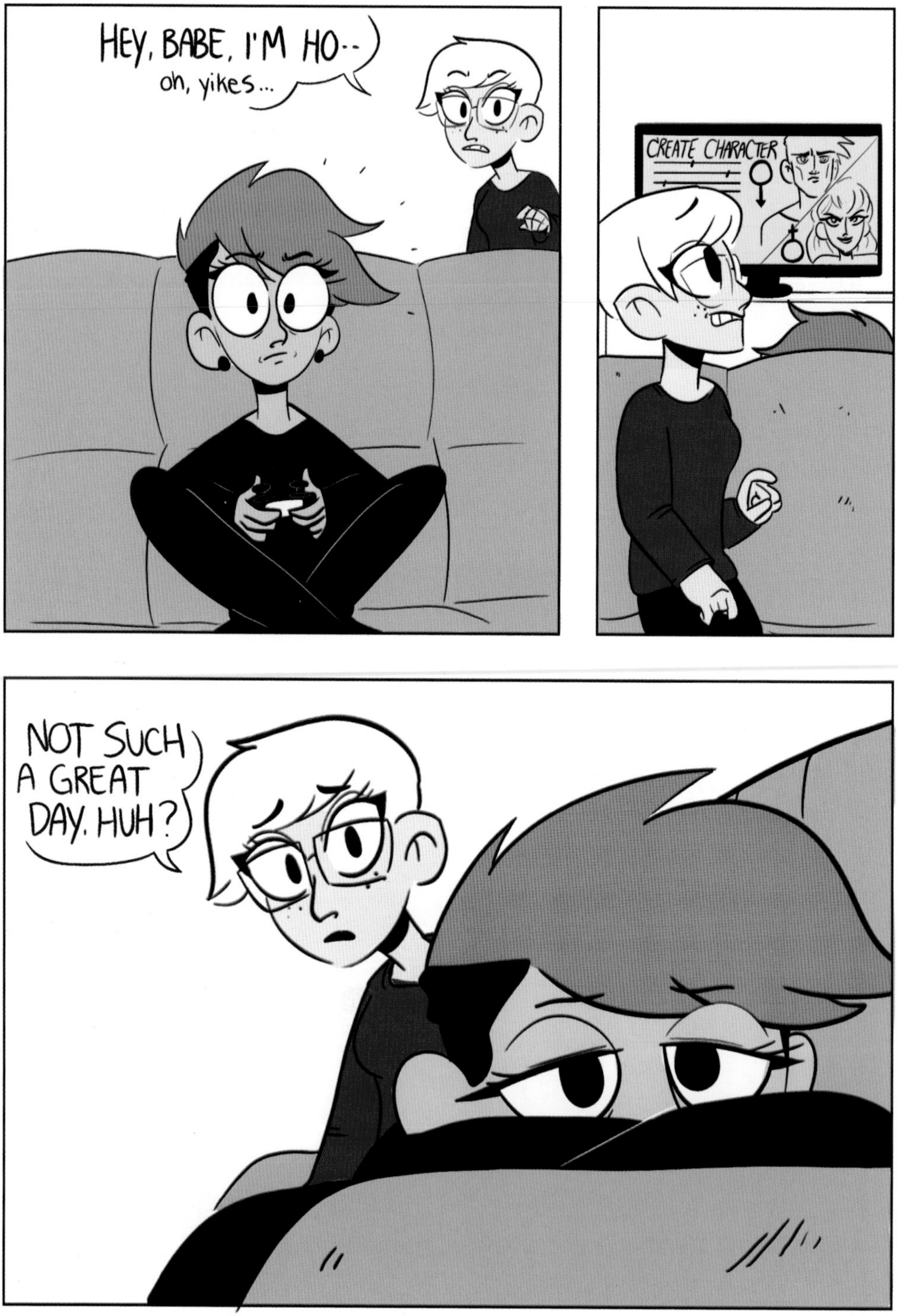
HEY, BABE, I'M HO--
oh, yikes...
CREATE CHARACTER
NOT SUCH A GREAT DAY. HUH?

GENDER THING?

MHM.

MISGENDERED THING?

YEP.

AH, CRUMBS...

MMF...

WELL, WHILE I DON'T UNDERSTAND FULLY WHAT YOU'RE GOING THROUGH, I DO GET HOW IMPORTANT IT IS TO FEEL VALID.

AND I'M NOT JUST SAYING THIS 'CAUSE I'M A PARTNER... BUT YOU'RE PRETTY. AND SUPER VALID.

AND I LOVE YOU AND... STUFF.

I KNOW. ♥

WHAT, YOU'RE HAN SOLO NOW? HOW ABOUT WE SEE WHAT KIND OF FREAK WE CAN MAKE WITH THIS CHARACTER CREATOR?

SOUNDS GREAT.

FIN 🎱

THE TAO OF DUCKY

Harris O'Malley

The night was pitch black as I trudged my way down the Texas hill-country back road, the stars shining as only they can in the middle of nowhere. In the distance, when the wind pitched just right, I could hear the sounds of my classmates carousing and the dull, barely audible thump of bass.

It was supposed to be the most important night of my life. Here I was lost on a godforsaken dirt road, inexorably making my way toward a conversation I desperately didn't want to have.

This was not how I pictured my movie ending.

I should probably back up a little, huh?

I was the quintessential awkward teen in high school. I was bookish and shy, far more interested in comics and fantasy than I was in things like, say, interacting with my peers. I had the kind of tan one can only achieve through a life devoted to video games and the social skills to match.

Of course, I had aspirations to coolness. However, my ambitions outstripped not just my reach but also my ideas of what might actually make me cool.

I sketched anime characters—at a time when anime was still "those weird titty cartoons" that you could only see at two a.m. or through fourth-hand fan-subbed copies—because I thought it made me deep. I studied martial arts under the assumption that being a badass would make me cool. I grew my hair into a ponytail because Duncan MacLeod had one in *Highlander: The Series.*

I had an unironic Three Wolf Moon shirt.

In short, my "coolness" could be defined as magical. That is: I made sex *disappear.*

And of course, I was determined that I was going to find love—or something like it—before I graduated. Or I would, if I had the slightest idea of what I was doing.

I knew what I *wanted*—love and sex, not necessarily in that order—but had no idea how to go about *getting* them. And as many a geek had done before me, I believed I had access to vaults of knowledge left unexplored by the mundanes around me.

Only those who were initiated into the secrets could understand the wisdom contained within. I was the seeker of truths kept hidden. *I* would delve deep and gain troves of knowledge that would lead me to become the Casanova I was destined to be.

(Because, like every fantasy-obsessed nerd, I believed in destiny because of course I did. I was every scrappy underdog, every put-upon farm boy ever. I was a nerd and nerds were supposed to inherit the glory, damn it.)

And so I turned to the only resources I had available to me in the eighties and nineties: the movies. I studied the oeuvre of John Hughes like it was holy writ. If it involved a scrappy, nerdy underdog and an out-of-his-league love interest, I pored over it. I studied every shred of romantic lore I could like conspiracy theorists studied the Zapruder film.

I worshiped at the altar of Anthony Michael Hall, prayed for the intervention of Ducky, patron saint of the Friend Zone.

(Okay, sure, they never actually got the girl *but that's not the point, damn it . . .*)

I would arm myself with this occult wisdom and win the heart of my beloved, "Name to Be Added Later."

It's not that I didn't have my heart set on any one person . . . In fact, I hoarded crushes like Howard Hughes hoarded urine in jars. I could fall in love three times in a month. Every unrequited crush was a CRIME TOO HORRIBLE TO BE BORNE.

While I loved as much as I thought I could, none lasted . . . not until Samantha.[1]

My love for Samantha was born on a sophomore school trip, where . . . she was nice to me. Sure, our conversations were stilted and awkward and never got beyond basic school gossip. Yeah, I had way more fun with another girl I befriended—sharing every meal and having conversations that lasted through the night.[2] She was nice . . . but Sam was my One True Love, a *passion to last the ages.*

Or it would, if I ever, y'know. Talked to her for more than five minutes.

See, my studies had taught me to be what TV Tropes would later term the Dogged Nice Guy. I couldn't muster up the guts to say anything to Sam that wasn't standard school banalities, but damn it I had love on my side and that meant I was the HERO.

So I would follow her around like a lost puppy. I grumped, sighed, and mean-mugged any dude who talked to her for longer than five seconds—from a distance, I mean, most of them could've kicked my ass—and waited for the sheer strength of my devotion to win her over. Because frankly, talking to her did sweet fuck-all for me.

My love for Sam was unshakable. Even my abortive attempt to lose my virginity to a girl I originally met on CompuServe did nothing to shake my devotion to her.

For two years I looked for my chance to ask her out. And while I was thwarted time and again by not being able to be in her presence and make my mouth work at the same time . . . I had a secret weapon.

See, while I didn't have the gift of gab—not with anyone I was attracted to, anyway—the bod, or the looks, I had *movies* on my side. And I knew that it would just take one night, one magical, perfect night where the stars would align and fate would smile and give me the relationship I deserved.

And that was the Graduation Party.

---

[1] Names and details changed to protect the innocent and also cover my butt from the lawyers.

[2] Ironically enough, she had her own unrequited crush on another student at the time. If life worked like the movies, we would have had an epic "help each other win our crushes" project that would have led to our falling in love. Instead, she hooked up with him the next year, then realized she didn't actually like him that much.

If movies—from *Sixteen Candles* to *Dazed and Confused*—had taught me anything, it was that Parties Were Magic. Whether it was prom or "Meet at the Moon Tower," capital-P Parties were sacred, liminal spaces where reality could change and miracles could be had if your love was pure.

And by God, mine was.

It was the end of our senior year and graduation loomed. My study of film narrative—combined with a nerd's faith in destiny—taught me that this was my time.

Sam was going to be throwing an epic rager party at her parents' place. Clearly it was a sign from the gods themselves. They were serving me up my future on a silver platter.

(In reality, it was logistics: Sam's house was in the middle of nowhere, far back enough from the roads that we weren't likely to a] annoy the neighbors and b] get busted by the cops.)

Never mind that I had been to a total of three high-school parties. Never mind that I still hadn't had any conversation of substance with Sam. As God was my witness, this would be the night of my Heartfelt Declaration of Love.

I left nothing to chance. I scripted exactly what I would say. I work-shopped my speech with my friends. I stood in the mirror—when I wasn't working my nunchucks—and practiced like I was giving my acceptance speech at the Oscars. The full training montage.

This was my *Rocky 3*. I had the Eye of the Tiger.

I was *ready*.

I was *not* ready.

It was the eve of graduation. The party was that night. I was bursting with nerves. I wanted to fly in every direction at once and vibrate through space and time. I stared at the clock like it was my enemy as seconds stretched into infinity. I prayed for time to slow the hell down as my nerves jangled like a Philip Glass song.

The drive to Sam's house seemed to take hours. It was on the outskirts of the county, but it may as well have been on Mars. Through twists and several wrong turns down dirt roads, I finally found my way up the winding driveway toward the promised land and the cars that lined its entrance.

By the time I arrived, the party was in full swing—kegs had been tapped and cans of Lone Star decorated the lawn like fallen soldiers. A fire had been built, making shadows dance. In the darkness of the trees, I could just make out the writhing forms of people who'd snuck away to make out. With luck, I might soon be joining them. With luck, Sam hadn't already.

The Graduation Party was the social mixer of the season. Boundaries fell as the beer flowed. Freshmen, sophomores, juniors, and seniors mixed freely while cliques disintegrated. The Queen Bees drank with the Stoners, and the Country Shit Kickers drunkenly sang along to Boyz II Men with the Mexican and Japanese students. Everyone was your best friend—a night of bonhomie and fraternity. It was perfect.

And I was *terrified*.

I took a reconnaissance lap around the party, eyeballing the guests, spotting my friends and—most of all—trying to make sure that Sam had not hooked up yet. She was single tonight, which was both blessing and curse. On the one hand, it meant that I still had my shot. On the other . . . well, so did everyone else.

I wasn't ready. I was one of only two sober people at this party; even my friends who were devoted teetotalers had cracked beers. And then it happened. I felt a hand reach into mine and pull me into a hug, words slurring in my ear about being glad to see me.

It was Vanessa—a sophomore I knew from shared classes. Adorable with her honey-gold hair, and evidently a touchy-feely drunk. We were friendly but not full-body-hug friendly—A-frame hugs at best. But as her arms wrapped around me, my resolve began to waver. Vanessa wasn't Sam . . . "But does that really matter?" whispered my treacherous, hormone-addled brain.

Of course, he who hesitates is lost; as I tried to think of a way to suggest that we adjourn to Make Out Woods, she danced off, leaving me both excited and confused.

I was torn; do I pursue what seemed to be a new and unexpected opportunity? Try to lose my virginity before graduation? Or do I stay true to my dream and my heart and follow the Tao of *Can't Hardly Wait*, the Zen of *Say Anything*?

In the end, the decision was made for me when I couldn't find Vanessa anywhere . . . nor could I find Sam. I sat at the fire pit, the lonely sober soul with cans of Dr Pepper as I scanned the perimeter and waited.

It was at midnight when my moment finally arrived. Sam emerged from the smokers' circle and rejoined the fray. I took a fortifying gulp of caffeine, screwed my courage to the sticking place, and marched toward her. "Hey," I said, smoothly.

"Hey, I'm so glad you came!" Sam chirped, leaning in to give me an A-frame hug. Did it linger just a hint longer than social convention called for? Was there a slight rocking that didn't accompany the Just a Friend hug? Clearly, it was time. I took her hand.

"Hey, can we talk for a moment?" I asked.

"Sure! What's up?" she said with a smile.

I looked around . . . I couldn't do this with an audience. Too many eyes glinted around the fire pit, watching me. Too many people knew my plan. "Er . . . in private?" I asked, leading her over to the line of cars by the entrance.

Standing next to my van, I took a deep breath. "Sam . . . I just wanted to tell you that I really, *really* like—"

"Do you think UFOs are real?" she asked.

That was so far off script that my brain vapor locked.

". . . I mean, I've had a thing for yo—"

"Because living out here I see, like, a *lot* of stuff in the sky and I know you're into *The X-Files* and stuff and you probably know about these things and do you ever just look at the sky and think, 'There's no way we're alone here,' but at the same time really like it's just us and the sky . . ."

Damn it, this was *not* what I'd planned. I tried again . . .

"I hope that you feel the same way for me and maybe if you do we could get into this car together and then we could . . . um . . ."

Even as the words tumbled out of my mouth, I wanted to dig a hole, jump in, and pull it in after me. Damn it, what the *fuck* was I saying? "I want to bang in the back seat" wasn't in the script!

She kept talking, seemingly not hearing me. I took another deep breath:

"Look, I love you. I've loved you since we first met. You're amazing. You're all I think of when I get up in the morning and the last thing I think of at night and . . ."

"But I mean, I'm glad you came and it's been so good to see you!" she said.

". . . Okay, well . . . I just had to tell you that."

There wasn't anything else to say. I got into my car. I'd said my piece. That was pretty damn cool. That was a great exit line. She'd remember that. I could leave on that note with my head held high, as awesome a cinema moment as one could like.

As I pulled out into the black Texas night, I realized: This wasn't *Pretty in Pink*, where even Ducky gets his day. This was *American Graffiti*, where a nerdy guy can get his moment of triumph and drive off to his awesome future. I threw it all out there. Nobody could take that from me. This would lead me into my college years of coolness. And maybe it would stick with Sam . . . And when I came back in the summer . . .

I was so caught up in these dreams of glory that I didn't see the ditch until my car dipped into it headfirst.

The party had wound down. Only stragglers remained, sprawled on outdoor furniture and in beds of pickup trucks. I picked my way around cigarettes in discarded cups, sighed, and knocked at the front door

Sam opened the door, eyes red and bleary with confusion.

I felt the last of my movie mojo shatter and crumble at my feet as I choked out the words:

"Hey, um . . . I need a ride home."

SO SAY WE ALL

BY LEVI HASTINGS

ACTION STATIONS! SET CONDITION ONE THROUGHOUT THE SHIP!

I FELL IN LOVE WITH **BATTLESTAR GALACTICA**.

I WAS SKEPTICAL AT FIRST: OF THIS SMALL TOWN, OF THIS CHARMING NEW GUY, AND MOST OF ALL, OF THIS SHOW HE KEPT TALKING ABOUT.

THAT RIDICULOUS 70S SHOW ABOUT SPACE ROBOTS?

YEAH, BUT THEY REIMAGINED THE WHOLE THING! AND IT'S NOT **REALLY** ABOUT ROBOTS IN SPACE. IT'S MORE OF A METAPHOR ABOUT OUR TECHNOLOGY GETTING THE BETTER OF US.

IT'S ALSO ABOUT TERRORISM AND TORTURE, POLITICAL VS. MILITARY FORCE, SURVIVAL, AND MORALITY, AND GRIEF, AND...

BUT SAM WAS DETERMINED TO GET ME ONBOARD.

ONLY A FEW DATES IN, AND I WAS ALREADY LOOKING FOR ANY EXCUSE TO SPEND TIME TOGETHER AT HIS PLACE.

YOU WANNA GIVE IT A SHOT?

SURE, LET'S GO FOR IT.

EVEN IF THAT MEANT WATCHING A SILLY SCI-FI REBOOT.

IT STARTED OUT A LITTLE CLUNKY AND LOW BUDGET, BUT THE PREMISE AND CHARACTERS WERE COMPELLING.

OH, I **LOVE** THIS PART.

WHAT DO YOU HEAR, STARBUCK?

NOTHIN' BUT THE RAIN, SIR.

I WAS MORE ENTERTAINED BY HIS ENTHUSIASM AND FLATTERED THAT HE WAS TRYING SO HARD TO IMPRESS ME.

MAYBE ONE MORE BEFORE BED?

THE SHOW BECAME OUR DATE-NIGHT RITUAL, AND I STARTED TO EQUATE THE DRUMBEATS OF THE OPENING CREDITS TO THE THUMPING OF MY EAGER HEART.

I SOON BEGAN TO DRAW THE PARALLELS BETWEEN OUR PROGRESS IN THE SHOW AND THE STAGES OF OUR RELATIONSHIP.

IF THEY'VE EVOLVED TO LOOK LIKE HUMANS, ANY ONE OF US COULD BE A CYLON.

I KNOW IT'S NOT IDEAL, BUT WE NEED TO BE CAREFUL WHO WE TELL ABOUT US.

THE GRITTY, RETRO AESTHETIC OF THE SHOW ECHOED THE RUNDOWN, INDUSTRIAL COASTAL TOWN IN WHICH I FOUND MYSELF STRANDED, TRYING TO MAKE A HOME IN A PLACE I DID NOT BELONG.

WE NEED TO KNOW JUST HOW MANY ARE HIDING AMONG THE FLEET.

NEWS TRAVELS FAST AROUND HERE.

IF THE WRONG PERSON FOUND OUT, I COULD LOSE MY JOB.

LIKE BALTAR--THE SERIES' DEVIOUS SCIENTIST--SAM HAD HIS OWN REMOTE DREAM HOUSE ON THE RIVER, WHERE WE COULD ESCAPE, FAR FROM THE PRYING EYES AND SMALL-MINDED GOSSIP OF A SMALL TOWN.

IF THEY EVER LEARN THE TRUTH, GAIUS, THEY'LL THROW YOU OUT THE AIRLOCK.

HERE WE ARE! MY OWN LITTLE PARADISE.

IN BOTH CASES, I WAS COMPLETELY HOOKED BY THE END OF THE FIRST SEASON.

BRING IT HERE, PEACHES!

FRAK!

THE ARROW OF APOLLO! THIS IS THE KEY TO FINDING EARTH.

YOU'RE HERE OFTEN ENOUGH, YOU MIGHT AS WELL HAVE YOUR OWN SET.

I WAS MADLY IN LOVE DESPITE THE BONE-DEEP KNOWLEDGE THAT THIS COULD NOT LAST.

I KNOW IN MY GUT THAT SETTLING ON NEW CAPRICA WILL BE A DISASTER FOR HUMANITY.

AND I WON'T SAY OTHERWISE JUST TO WIN AN ELECTION.

LAST SWIM OF THE SUMMER. I'M NOT READY FOR IT TO END.

≶SIGHHH≶

ME NEITHER.

BECAUSE THIS WILL PROBABLY BE OUR LAST.

BY SEASON 3, IT BECAME CLEAR THAT SOME HARD CHOICES HAD TO BE MADE.

THERE'S ONLY ONE WAY THIS MISSION ENDS...

WITH THE SUCCESSFUL RESCUE OF OUR PEOPLE FROM THIS PLANET.

I CAN'T STAY HERE.

I LOVE YOU, BUT... I JUST CAN'T LIVE LIKE THIS.

THIS TOWN IS SO SMALL AND I CAN'T KEEP PRETENDING WE'RE JUST FRIENDS.

I KNOW I'M ASKING TOO MUCH.

YOU WOULD SHRIVEL UP AND DIE IF YOU STAYED HERE. AND I WON'T LET YOU DO THAT, EVEN FOR ME.

BUT THIS IS MY HOME. I CAN'T LEAVE.

IT WILL BE HARD FOR BOTH OF US, BUT DEEP DOWN WE ALWAYS KNEW THIS WASN'T FOREVER.

BY THE END OF THE SERIES, THE SHOW HAD RUN OFF THE RAILS, BUT WE MANAGED TO BRIDGE THE GAP BETWEEN ROMANCE AND FRIENDSHIP.

HOW 'BOUT THAT FINALE?

I'M SO MAD. I DON'T EVEN WANT TO TALK ABOUT IT.

LET'S JUST PRETEND THAT LAST SEASON NEVER HAPPENED.

WE BOTH MOVED ON WITH OUR LIVES AND REMAINED GOOD FRIENDS DESPITE OUR DISTANCE.

SO...HOW ARE THINGS GOING WITH ROB?

OH...GOOD. I...UH, TOOK HIM DOWN TO THE CABIN FOR THE FIRST TIME LAST WEEKEND.

THE YEARS BROUGHT US NEW LOVE, ADVENTURES, AND OBSESSIONS.

You're INVITED!

ALL OF WHICH WE EAGERLY SHARED WITH ONE ANOTHER.

UNTIL:

CAROL

HEY, I SAW YOUR MESSAGE. WHAT'S WRONG?

IT'S ABOUT SAM...

HE HAD A STROKE.

THEY'VE FLOWN HIM TO PORTLAND. HE'S IN THE ICU.

IT'S...NOT LOOKING GOOD.

YOU SHOULD COME AS SOON AS YOU CAN...

IF YOU WANT TO SAY GOODBYE.

I DROVE DOWN TO SAY MY FAREWELL.

BY THEN, THERE WAS NOTHING TO BE DONE BUT ABSORB THE SHOCK...

...AND AWAIT THE INEVITABLE.

I WAS ADRIFT IN A TERRIBLE LIMBO WAITING FOR NEWS OF HIS WORSENING CONDITION...

SO I SOUGHT COMFORT IN THE ONLY PLACE I COULD: BACK WHERE IT ALL BEGAN.

THE CYLONS WERE CREATED BY MAN

THIS HAS ALL HAPPENED BEFORE.

AND IT WILL ALL HAPPEN AGAIN.

THE FIRST MOMENTS UNLOCKED A FLOODGATE OF MEMORIES, TRANSPORTING ME BACK TO THAT REFUGE IN THE OREGON WOODS.

I ORIGINALLY LOVED THE SHOW FOR ITS COMPLEX POLITICS AND MORAL DILEMMAS, BUT ALL I COULD SEE NOW WERE THE THEMES OF GRIEF, REGRET, MORTALITY, AND HUMAN FRAILTY. I WAS HOOKED ALL OVER AGAIN.

WHAT CAN I GET FOR YOU?

A NEW BODY.

MAYBE ONE OF THOSE PRETTY BLOND CYLON MODELS.

IT PROVIDED A BRIEF ESCAPE FROM MY DESPAIR AND A WORTHY FOCUS FOR MY VIGIL.

ON THE MEMORY OF THOSE LYING HERE BEFORE YOU, WE SHALL FIND EARTH, AND IT SHALL BECOME OUR NEW HOME!

SO SAY WE ALL!

THEY TOOK HIM OFF LIFE SUPPORT THIS MORNING.

HE'S GONE.

SO SAY WE ALL!

SO SAY WE ALL!

WHAT DO YOU HEAR, STARBUCK?

NOTHIN' BUT THE RAIN, SIR.

IMMORTAL LOVE, FIRST EDITION

Katie West, illustration by Jamie McKelvie

I was born seven years after Anne Rice first released her classic *Interview with the Vampire* and I was a godless child. I have always believed that when you die, you're worm food and that's the extent of it. There is nothing more and nothing better waiting for me. I guess it follows that when I was seventeen years old, I read *The Vampire Lestat* and fell in love. A fictional character who believed only in himself and would never die? Lestat was everything I needed.

He was difficult, stubborn, and aloof, all characteristics I imagined were strengths that I possessed. Loving Lestat was an attempt to love myself, giving me permission to worship myself and fuck whatever comes after. But Lestat was also reckless, charming, and immortal, characteristics I decidedly did not possess. Loving Lestat was an attempt to punish myself, too, reminding myself that I would never be enough, know enough, love enough, do enough before I died and my one life was wasted. So I did the only thing that made sense: I started collecting copies of *Interview with the Vampire*, using my search for first editions and rare editions as atonement for my inability to live a life the love of my life, Lestat, would be proud of.

Sometimes I wonder if it was my anxiety over the seeming meaninglessness of this life that pushed me from one person's arms into the next's bed before anything could get too stable or too content. It wasn't so much fear of stability and commitment as fear of missing out. How could I be reckless and charming and Lestat-like with only a few lovers? Despite not being an immortal rock star vampire, I could still live hard and make my time count. For much of my life, this meant loving widely and fucking indiscriminately, and when that failed to produce a sense of accomplishment, buying more copies of *Interview with the Vampire*.

I bought a copy when I was in Montreal for my best friend's thirtieth birthday. The book is the only French-language edition in my collection, but I don't read French. The night before I bought it, I had left my husband at the hotel and gone out to a bar where my friends and I drank every drink on the menu. Twice. The morning after I took self-portraits in the February sun and in every one of them I looked sad. Often I wondered if my husband could read what I was saying in my self-portraits; half the time I was telling him I was looking for happiness, half the time I was talking about how I'd need to find it somewhere else. A month later my husband and I separated. A month later Jamie and I started dating.

When Jamie and I were half a year into our long-distance relationship, we met in New York City. On the morning I left, I saw a copy of *Interview with the Vampire* in a shop window. I was on my way to the airport, but texted Jamie in a panic from the cab, telling him about the book, how it looked like a first edition (it wasn't), could he go get it? It was six a.m., but he told me he'd look later. A couple of months after this, I texted Jamie again in a panic. I was sure the weight of the long distance was crushing me, I couldn't take the lack of intimacy, the five-hour time difference, the missing out on each other's lives. Jamie sent me a selfie of himself holding that book. I guessed I could last a few more months.

Six months later, I moved to London and it was not easy for me. I missed my friends, my family, my job, the sense of worth those things gave me. I missed understanding the cultural references, the politics, the comedy of the place where I lived. I explored the city a lot on my own because Jamie had to work long hours, long days. I was wandering in a Waterstones in central London when I saw it—a UK first edition, signed by Anne Rice. I didn't have a job, I didn't have any money, but I needed this book! I told Jamie about it and he gave me the money to buy it. I took his money because I felt he owed me. I'd left my life for him and I felt that made me entitled to this £150 signed UK first edition of *Interview with the Vampire*. It took longer than I'd like to admit to realize I owed him.

I have a copy from a shop in Port Elgin, a place I've been to every summer since I was born. The shop is half music, half books, with exactly the amount of Danielle Steele and Baby-Sitters Club books you would imagine in a cottage country full of retirees and grandparents. It's the place where I had my first boyfriend, my first kiss, where I learned to swim, where my ex-husband proposed to me, where I brought new boyfriends to determine if we were gonna make it. Did they love the sunsets as much as I did? Did they love the beach fries as much as I did? Did they understand the magic of this place where I grew into who I am today? In January Jamie starts telling me he's excited for our annual trip to Port Elgin in August. That's eight months of anticipation. He understands.

We went to Portland last year and one day we paid what we thought was much too much money to go to the Chinese gardens. It ended up being one of the best days I'd had for a long time. We spent hours in there, sitting in the teahouse, walking the gardens, enjoying the silence of each other. And every time I looked over at him, my heart felt too big for my chest. His hand found mine idly, without effort. He leaned in, face ducking out of the sun, into the shadow of my neck, his lips warm. I realized he'd taught me some eternal language, one I had thought myself fluent in, but content is not the same as happy. Afterward, we walked to Powell's City of Books and I bought two copies of *Interview with the Vampire*.

I own sixteen copies of *Interview with the Vampire*, one for every year I've spent searching for a life that would feel like enough, a life where, when it came time for me to be worm food, I'd gladly accept that dark dirt into my mouth. And though Lestat may no longer be the vampire who once inspired me, challenged me, and made me swoon, he was instrumental in bringing me toward this life I now live with a man who inspires me, challenges me, and makes me swoon every damned day. For a book I've never read, that's not half bad.

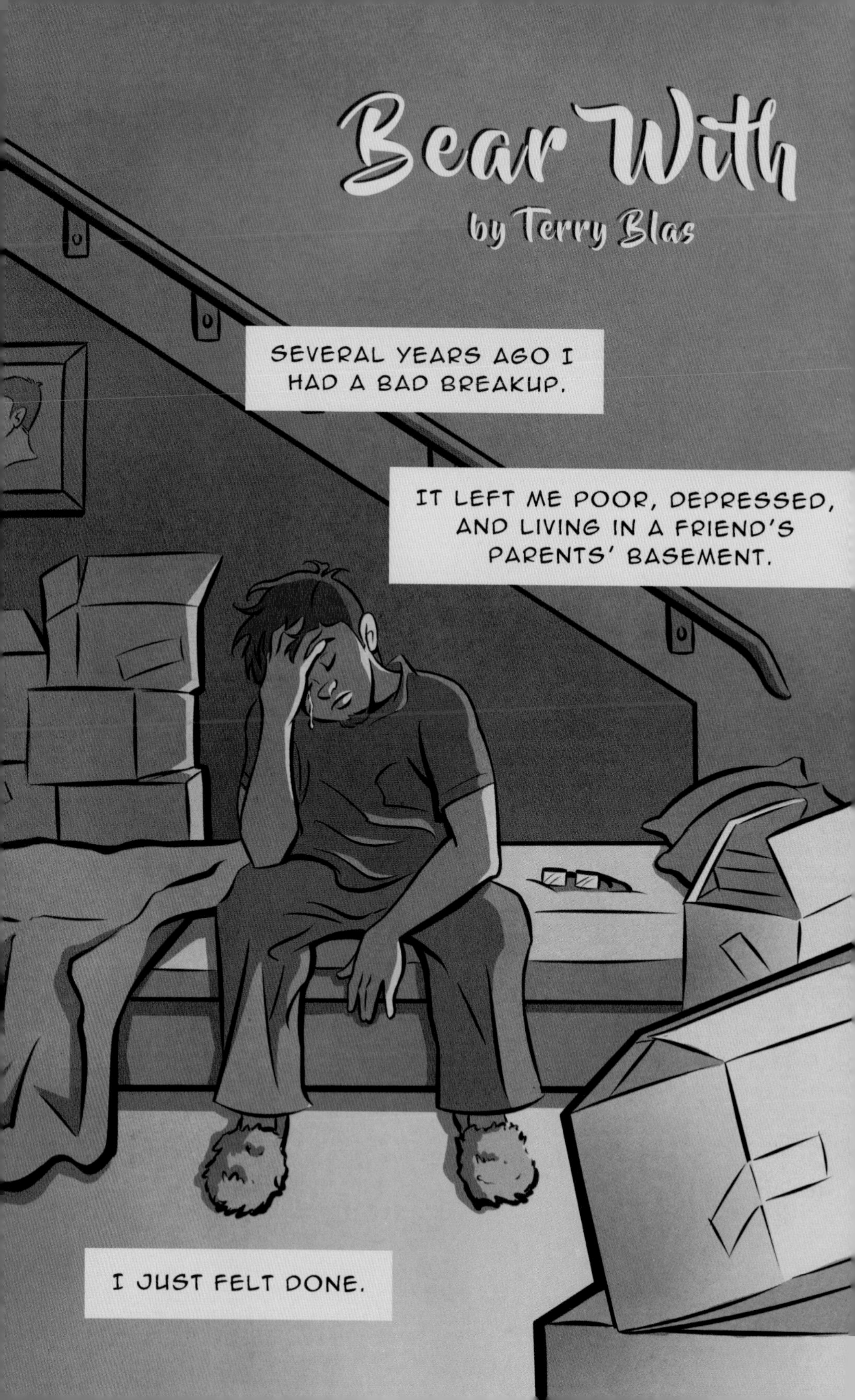
Bear With
by Terry Blas
SEVERAL YEARS AGO I HAD A BAD BREAKUP.
IT LEFT ME POOR, DEPRESSED, AND LIVING IN A FRIEND'S PARENTS' BASEMENT.
I JUST FELT DONE.

I TOLD MY FRIEND **BEN** THAT I DIDN'T THINK I'D DATE AGAIN.

OH, I DON'T THINK THAT'S TRUE.

EVER.

SELF-DOUBT CREPT IN.

I'M SUCH A NERD. I COLLECT ACTION FIGURES AND UNICORNS.

I MAKE COMICS.

I'VE NEVER REALLY HAD MUCH LUCK WITH GUYS.

MOST GUYS THAT I HAVE DATED ENDED UP CALLING ME

FAT.

CONSIDERING ALL OF THIS, I DON'T KNOW WHAT PROMPTED ME TO, BUT I SET UP AN *OKCUPID* PROFILE.

PRETTY QUICKLY I FOUND A REALLY CUTE GUY WHO ALSO LIKED BRITISH TV.

I DIDN'T THINK HE'D GO OUT WITH ME.

SCOTT
ENGLAND
DOCTOR WHO

HAVE YOU EVER SEEN *MIRANDA?*

THAT DID THE TRICK.

HI! I'M *SCOTT.*

SORRY, I DIDN'T KNOW WHERE TO PARK.

I'M *TERRY.*

I UH... I MADE YOU A *HEATHER SMALL.*

WE STARTED DATING.

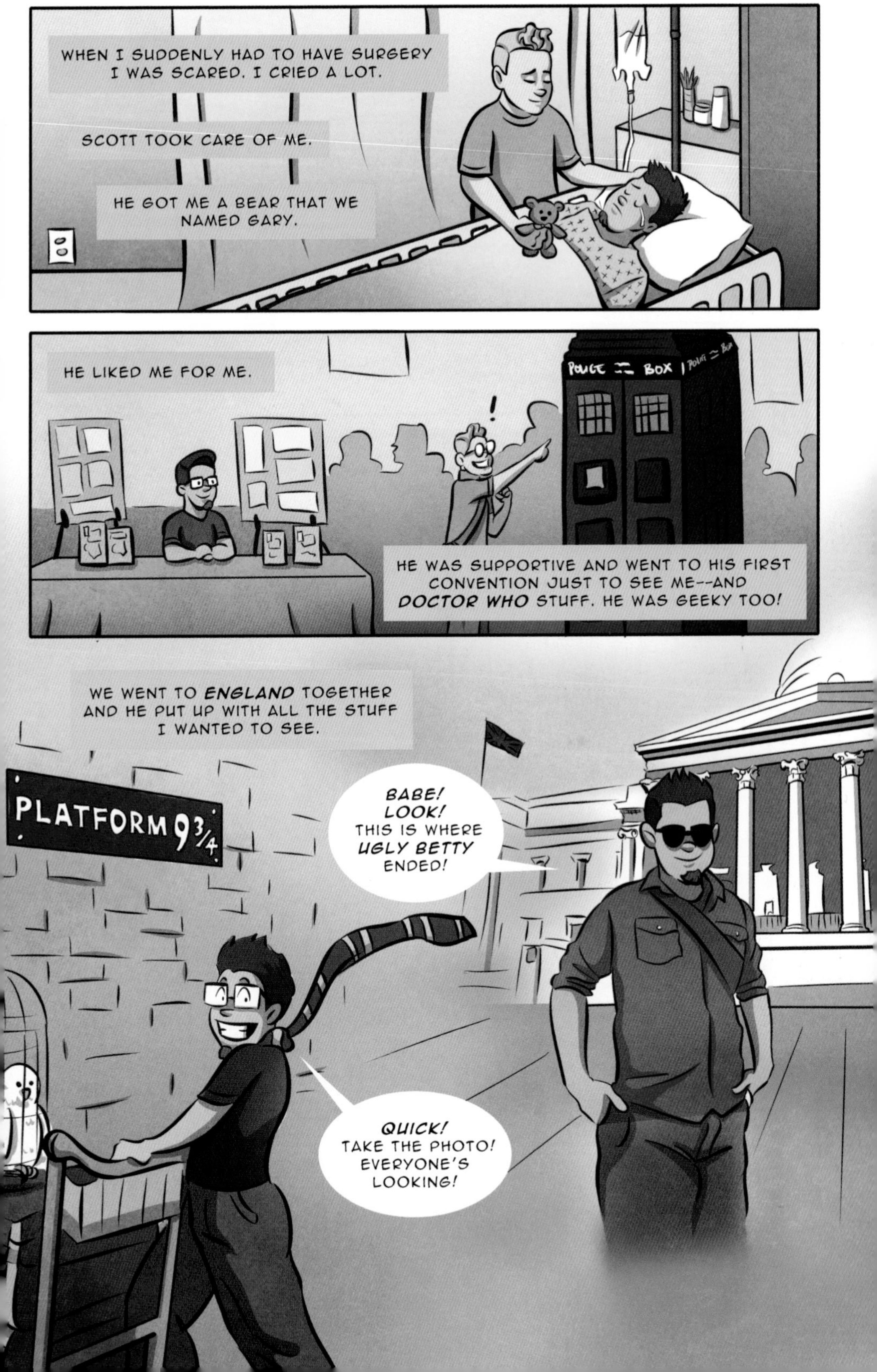
WHEN I SUDDENLY HAD TO HAVE SURGERY I WAS SCARED. I CRIED A LOT.
SCOTT TOOK CARE OF ME.
HE GOT ME A BEAR THAT WE NAMED GARY.
HE LIKED ME FOR ME.
POLICE BOX
HE WAS SUPPORTIVE AND WENT TO HIS FIRST CONVENTION JUST TO SEE ME--AND *DOCTOR WHO* STUFF. HE WAS GEEKY TOO!
WE WENT TO *ENGLAND* TOGETHER AND HE PUT UP WITH ALL THE STUFF I WANTED TO SEE.
PLATFORM 9 3/4
BABE! LOOK! THIS IS WHERE *UGLY BETTY* ENDED!
QUICK! TAKE THE PHOTO! EVERYONE'S LOOKING!

AND THEN ONE NIGHT, AFTER HE TOOK ME TO HEAR A SYMPHONY PLAY A SET OF *DISNEY* MUSIC...

HE ASKED ME TO MARRY HIM AND SAID HE WANTED TO TAKE MY NAME AS HIS.

I WAS SO HAPPY AND COULD HARDLY REMEMBER EVER BEING SAD.

I BEGAN TO FEEL LIKE I NEVER SHOULD HAVE LET MYSELF DOUBT THAT SOMEONE WONDERFUL WOULD LOVE ME DESPITE MY GEEKINESS.

THAT THOSE QUALITIES MIGHT BE GREAT ASPECTS OF MY PERSONALITY THAT SOMEONE WOULD APPRECIATE.

LOVEOO.

BECAUSE THAT'S *EXACTLY* WHAT HAPPENED.

THE WHITE GLOVE BRIGADE

Kristian Bruun

Is it strange that for a very long time my ideal woman came in the shape of a lingerie model? Or from a comic book? Or a *Playboy* for that matter? Is this different than most teenage boys? Not really. It's not realistic, of course—I *think* I knew that then, but I was at an all-boys military school in the pre-internet age and finding a woman in the flesh to daydream over was damn hard to do. Same-sex education is the worst possible place for hetero-sex education. How do you learn about women in an environment almost completely devoid of them?

Looking back on my four years of military high school I realize how much that single-sex society affected my romantic future. High school is supposed to be the place where you learn to fall flat on your face when it comes to dating and sex. You experiment on how to ask someone out, how to attempt making moves on someone, and most importantly you fail. Sometimes a lot. Take a whole gender out of the equation (if that's what you're into), add to it exploding hormones and a thirsty sex drive, and you have a recipe for sexual frustration of prison proportions. Necessity is the mother of invention, however, and some of us became pretty resourceful.

Leave was everything. Leave was the only time you were allowed off campus—only on certain days within certain hours and only if you were in good standing with the school (academics, discipline, etc.). It was a cadet's chance to taste freedom, to feel what it was like to be a normal high-school kid—well, minus the fact that we had to be in uniform the whole time so everyone else around us knew where we went to school. We could only go to two places while on leave: the small town thirty minutes' walk from school or the King of Prussia Mall (at the time the second-largest mall in America). The town was used to the sight of little gray soldiers walking around, filling up on pizza, hoagies, and junk food (the food was terrible at the school). The crafty cadets knew where to buy porn and cigarettes (to sell back at the barracks) and if you went behind any building in that town you could probably find them chain-smoking menthols. Ultimately, leave was where the girls were and for that you went to the mall. Where else would girls want to hang out in the midnineties? This was the decade that gave us classics like *Mallrats* and *Clueless*, after all. We had a special short bus that would drive us back and forth on the weekends after chapel and parade. We would cram into the bus in uniform and bounce back and forth as it weaved its way through the curving, forested roads that emptied out across freeways to the mall.

There was only one problem: high-school girls weren't into awkward dorks in uniform. Only the cool kids could talk to the girls. You know the kind, the ones who were sent to military school as a punishment and oozed this strange "I don't give a shit about anything" confidence, while the rest of us watched in envy, paralyzed by the fear of rejection. So here I was in a mall full of cute girls and there was nothing I could do. In fact, only very recently have I come to realize that I have a crippling fear of starting conversations. It's strange, I know. I'm an actor; I'm used to interviews and interactions with strangers on the street, but the idea of *starting* a conversation with someone sends me into flop sweats and butterflies. I just simply can't go up to someone and start talking. If they come to *me* and start a conversation I'm totally fine, but what high-school girl approaches some cadet in uniform to have a chat? It just didn't happen. It was unheard of.

So instead there would be a steady stream of cadets walking into Frederick's of Hollywood to pretend to browse the lingerie for their "girlfriend" until they got close enough to the cash register to grab a catalog and beat a hasty retreat. I've always wondered what went through the minds of the women who worked there. Maybe they took pity on us. Sometimes they would let us take an extra one for a friend. With sexy catalogs tucked into our uniformed jackets, we would pile onto the bus and head back to prison, most of us having only talked to each other, disappointed but still happy to have escaped campus for a few hours.

The other sources of "inspiration" were either comic books, loaded with images of buxom babes kicking ass, or actual porno mags, acquired from a shady establishment that would sell to baby-faced cadets. The key was to not get caught, of course, and hiding porn became an exercise in espionage—we were underage; pornography was considered contraband. You could risk it by pulling out your bottom desk drawer and hiding the mags under there, in the hope that room inspectors wouldn't be that thorough, or you could DIY a secret shelf or compartment that no one knew existed if you climbed behind your desk. Comics and lingerie catalogs technically had no nudity and were therefore safe. Ish.

I can't remember another time in my life when I was so desperately horny. I would sit in class with a painful erection in my gray wool pants (everyone did) and when class was over I would hold my bag in front of me as I navigated to my next class—only to sit there, my mind drifting through the memorized lingerie catalog or *X-Men* comic sitting in my desk drawer back at the barracks.

A few times a year the school would hold dances and girls from neighboring towns and schools would arrive by the busload. What parent would let their daughter come to one of these things?! What would proceed was the most awkward display of fear and sexual frustration. The cool boys would be fine, of course, but the rest of us would just dance in a sweaty circle with each other. We all became great dancers, protected by our cadet brothers as we took turns in the center of the circle trying out break dance moves that would crack everyone up. The jocks, funny kids, nerds, officers, sergeants, and privates would all awkwardly band together, secure in our fraternity, and glance longingly at the girls, most of whom danced with themselves. The odd cool cadet would be confidently grinding up against one, and eventually they would disappear to the bushes or "go for a walk." Oh how we all longed to "go for a walk." The majority of us just went back to the barracks, tired and sweaty. If you were lucky your roommate had leave and was gone for the weekend, or you didn't care and jerked off silently in your bunk.

Which brings me to the act. Most adults know it well—teenage boys certainly do; we were pros. Masturbation was more than just an exercise in orgasm; it was stress relief, it was meditation, it was our daily (sometimes twice or thrice daily) prayer to ourselves. Eight hundred boys deep in the throes of puberty. It was the easiest outlet. It even became a game. Catching someone in the act was the second-greatest satisfaction. Our doors had electronic keypads on them and if you could type the code in quickly enough you could burst through the door in two seconds, not enough time for one to cover himself. If you screwed up the code the door would lock for five seconds, and thus your chance at catching your roommate doing the hand dance would be ruined.

It happened to everyone eventually. It was simple statistics. I had a free period one day and made my way back to the barracks for an afternoon prayer session. I checked my roommate's schedule on his corkboard—yes, he had class! Five minutes later I was seated at my desk with my pants around my ankles, porno mag open in front of me, bottle of moisturizer out—I couldn't look any more like the poster child for masturbation. I heard a succession of rapid beeps and the door burst open. All I had time to do was pull the desk drawer out over my lap with my free hand.

"Hey . . . whatcha doin' there?" my roommate asked, looking over my shoulder.

"Um. I was . . . uh . . . I thought you had class?"

"Teacher was sick," he said as he sat down with his back to me. He didn't move, just left me there in my shame. I sheepishly wiped the moisturizer off my hands and shuffled my pants back up, busted. Now there was a tradition within the corps of cadets that anyone caught masturbating had to wear a white glove on the offending hand. We had a lot of white gloves—we wore them for Sunday parades. I got lucky that day; my roommate didn't enforce that tradition. He kept my shame in the room.

At my recent twenty-year reunion we traded tales of catching so-and-so doing it under his desk, what's-his-name caught using a black dress sock for the act, and someone else caught late at night in the showers. There was the time that guy marched down the hallway wearing nothing but parade belts and a sword, his massive schwanz swinging like a pendulum while he called out commands as we killed ourselves laughing. Thank god this was before digital cameras. We were comfortable with our bodies in a way I've never seen anywhere else. You had to be. Our latrines were a row of toilets with no doors on them, so you only had a divider between each one. Five shower heads in a row. Latrine activities were a communal affair and our most private moments often got dragged into the light. Someone at reunion pointed out that only at military school could you know what everyone's penis looked like.

I'm sure you're wondering by now, but I did eventually manage to "go for a walk" with someone. It was my senior year and I was hooked up with a blind date for one of our proms. Sadly I've forgotten her name, but she was cute and sweet and seemed to like me. There I was, an officer in full dress uniform (black pants with a red stripe down the side, gray wool tunic with medals, ranks, and a red silk sash), and there she was, pretty in her light blue formal dress. We danced closer and closer as the night wore on and before long she asked me if I wanted to take a walk; the dance was about to end and we clearly didn't want the night to end.

We decided to head toward the football field at the back of the campus. I was convinced we would see other couples there but to my surprise we were alone. We didn't even sit on the bleachers, we sat on the ground—maybe we were more out of sight that way. To be gentlemanly I took off my tunic for us to sit on. And then we made out. For a very long time. Groping each other in our formalwear. I was excited and terrified at the same time. I didn't know how to proceed—what would be too forward? I didn't have any condoms. Did she want to go that far? Eventually we both were so riled up we had to part ways because clearly I wasn't going to make any further moves. We said good night, and I went back to the barracks disappointed and thrilled at the same time.

I don't remember seeing her again. I think we promised to hang out, but it was the end of the year and I was graduating and heading back to Canada so we both knew that wasn't very likely. It was a magical, frustrating night and I always wished I had a chance to explore what could've been. Instead I had years of sheepish dating before I discovered who I was and started living like it.

Today, my old school is co-ed. I remember the uproar when they were considering it—the alumni whining about "tradition" and the problems that would arise from having women around. They were probably just jealous they didn't have girls when they were there. And I admit, I was reluctant at first too, but that didn't last long. If school is supposed to prepare you for the real world, wouldn't you want to be in an environment that best *emulated* the real world? Fuck tradition. Today's military is co-ed. *Life* is co-ed. I can't help but think if military school was co-ed when I was there I might not have needed to make those visits to

Frederick's of Hollywood, wouldn't have needed to spend years trying to figure out how to talk to women. I could've gone for multiple walks to the football field. Or maybe I'd still have been the shy kid afraid to talk to girls, reading comic books and dreaming of unrealistically proportioned women. Still, I would've loved the chance to find out.

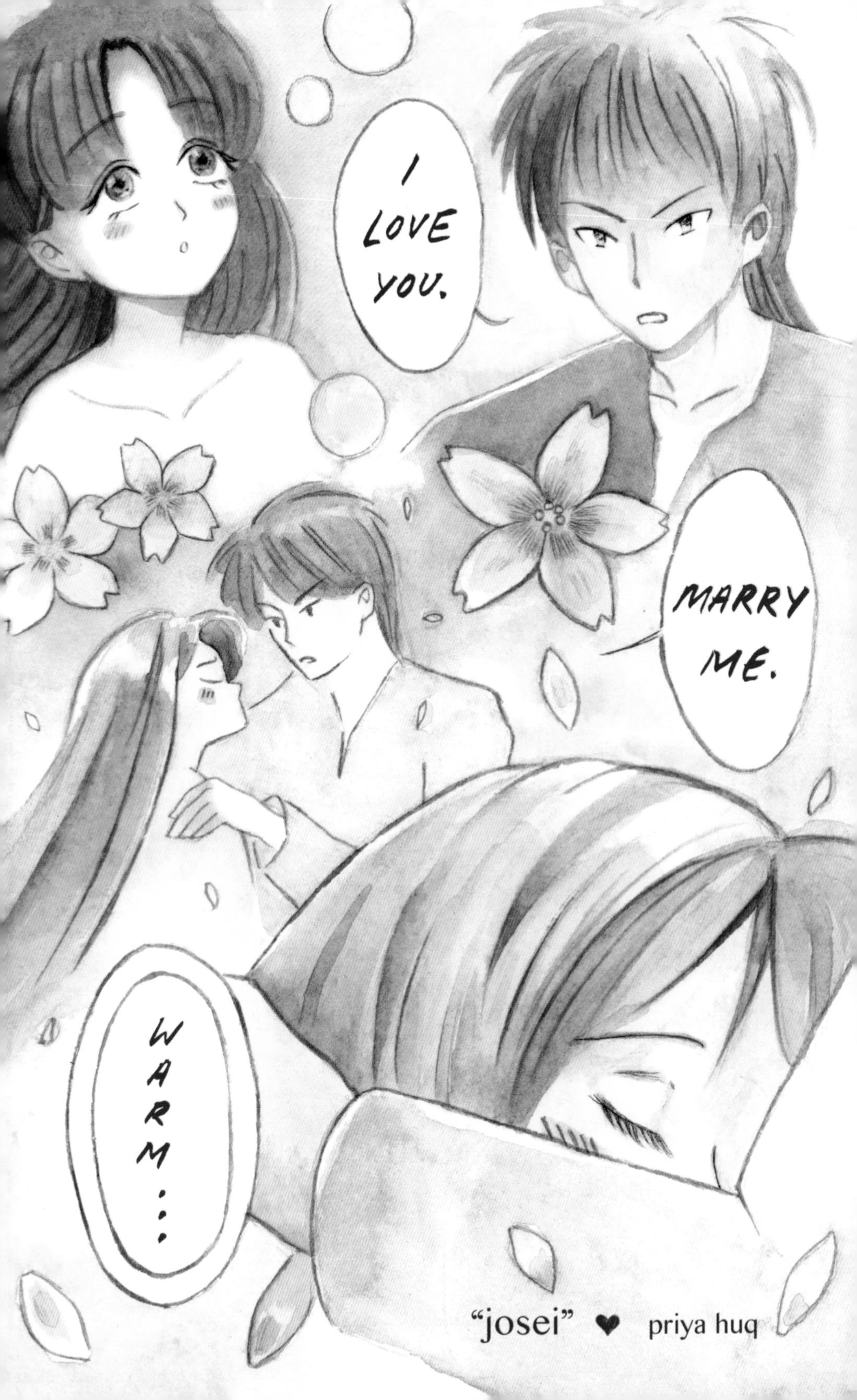
I LOVE YOU.
MARRY ME.
WARM...

"josei" ♥ priya huq

this comic is SO GOOD!!

Maybe...

Ahem!

Someday!!

I'm giving you detention.

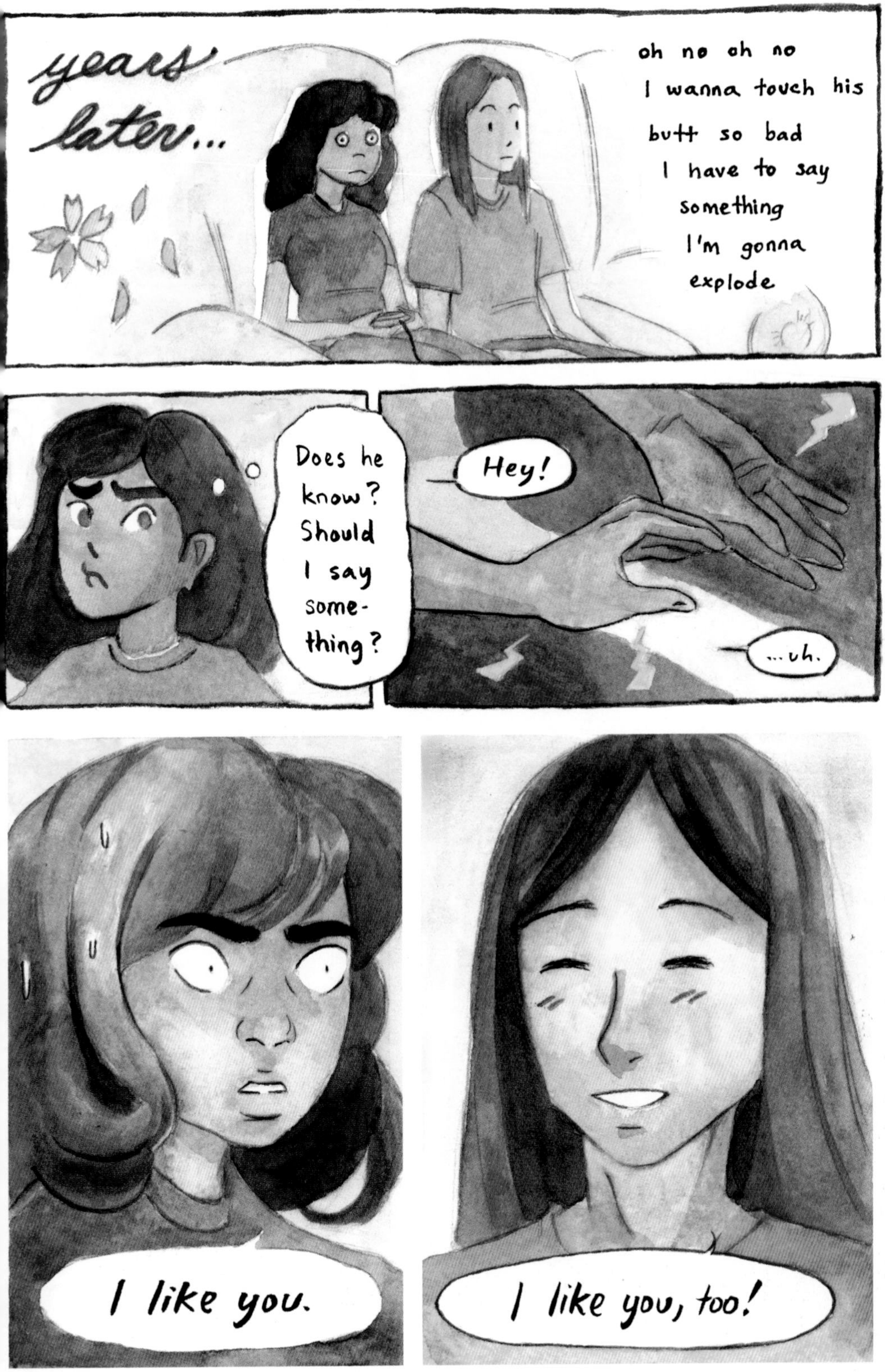
years later...
oh no oh no I wanna touch his butt so bad I have to say something I'm gonna explode
Does he know? Should I say some-thing?
Hey!
...uh.
I like you.
I like you, too!

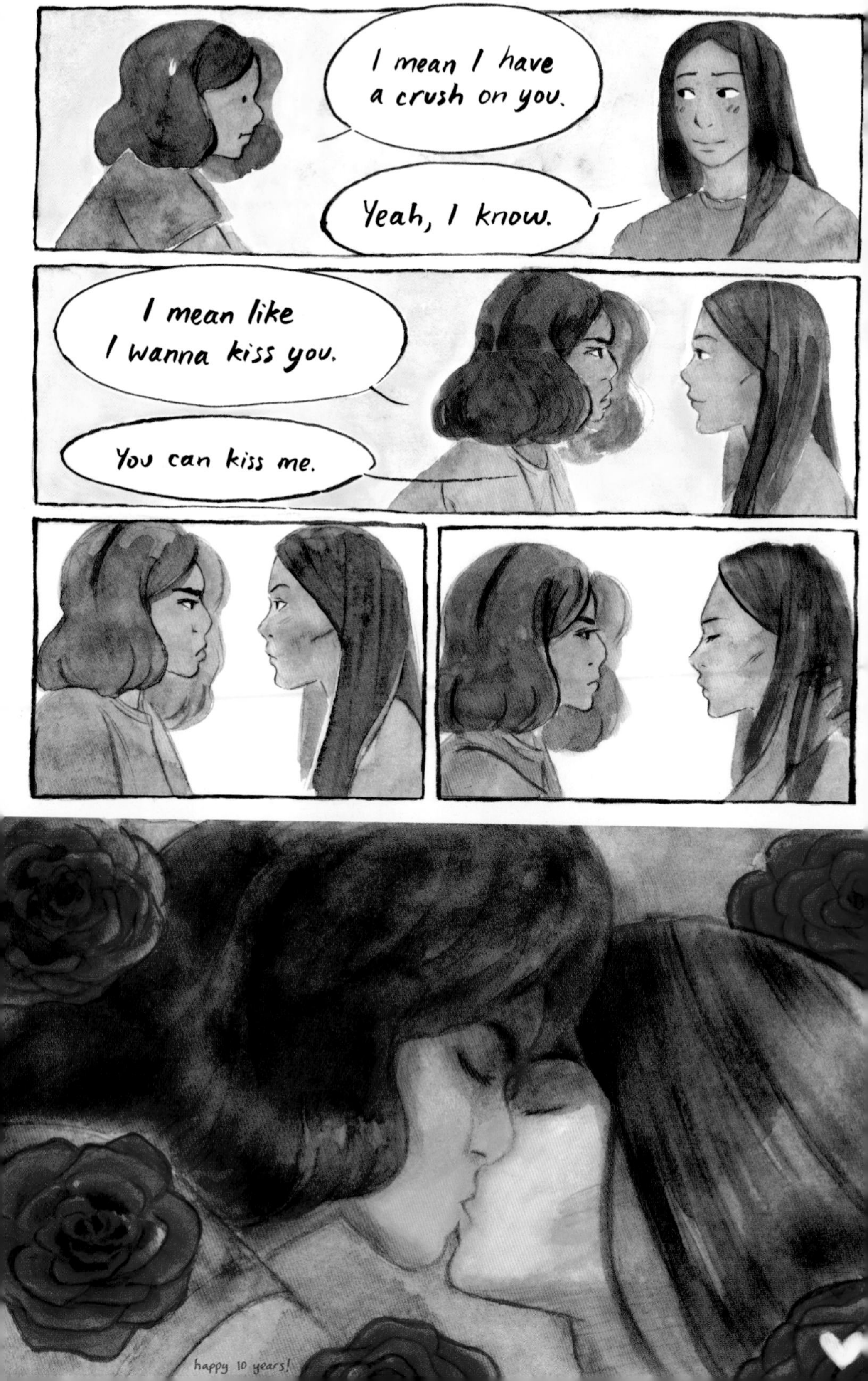
I mean I have a crush on you.
Yeah, I know.
I mean like I wanna kiss you.
You can kiss me.
happy 10 years!

I was 20 years old, underemployed, and about to flunk out of art school. But luckily, this...

COOL CHICK

...was my girlfriend.

story & art by Ryan Dunlavey

Frankie was my first girlfriend who actually *liked* the same stuff I did -- comic books, sci-fi, art, punk rock -- long before being a "geek" was considered normal.

She was cute, personable, *hilarious*, and unlike anyone I'd *ever* met before.

I fell for her hard and fast.

And she seemed to like me a lot too.

It was never just a crush. I'd had girlfriends before but not like Frankie. Being with her just came so naturally and easily, and for the first time in my life, it felt like *love* -- for real.

We spent *all* our free time together and she was the one part of my life that I felt like I *hadn't* screwed up.

But we were two rookies -- both still living with our parents, unsure of what kind of grownups we would be.

But there was *another* problem...

I was *not* cool, and Frankie *totally* was.

Frankie was naturally charismatic and made friends easily...

...I struggled to just *participate* in conversations.

(Still do.)

We had great one-on-one chemistry, but in social situations I was a *disaster*.

She had also had **loads** of youthful rebellious adventures. Raising hell, breaking rules, pulling pranks... and **always** getting away with it.

Not me, not once. I had spent most of my high-school weekends with the same guys I ate lunch with every day -- at the arcade, reading comics, playing D&D.

Ironically, Frankie ALSO played D&D, but I didn't click with her group and they never invited me in.

HEY LOOK, GUYS, I DREW YOUR CHARACTERS!

GUYS?

The times I spent around her family and sprawling collections of friends caused an ever-increasing series of pained groans and eye rolls.

WAIT... **YOU'RE** GOING OUT WITH **HER**? REALLY?!

After a year the romance had cooled and I was sure Frankie was going to dump me. I was desperate not to lose her **and** it was starting to show, which didn't help.

I had the urge to impress her, thinking maybe she would like me more... and it had to be SOON.

The boyfriend role I **excelled** at was the all-purpose sidekick -- going to events, running errands, etc.

Like this day when we returned a well-meaning relative's **horrible** Christmas present.

I hadn't even gotten her a gift -- partially because I was broke, but mostly because I was scared I would give her something lame.

NO-- YOU HAVE TO GO TO **CUSTOMER SERVICE** TO MAKE RETURNS.

DO I NEED A RECEIPT? CAUSE IT WAS BOUGHT AT A AUFMANN'S IN PITTSBUR--

AS LONG AS THE TAG IS STILL ON IT AND IT'S STILL IN STOCK HERE AT THIS STORE, YOU CAN RETURN IT FOR *CASH.*

The cashier's explanation gave me an idea.

HOLD UP. I WANNA TRY SOMETHING...

WHAT DO YOU HAVE *THAT* FOR?

WE'RE GONNA *DOUBLE* YOUR CHRISTMAS GIFT.

DO YOU WANT CASH OR CREDIT?

CASH, PLEASE.

SERVICE

OKAY, THESE WENT ON SALE TODAY SO I CAN ONLY GIVE YOU $20 FOR EACH --CREDIT WILL GIVE YOU THE FULL $28 EACH.

UM, CASH IS FINE!

...AND 40. HAVE A HAPPY HOLIDAY!

HOLY SHIT, THAT WAS *AWESOME!*

I couldn't believe it worked.

Kaufmann's

This was it. This was my big chance to be "The Cool Boyfriend." For once.

WE NEED TO DO THAT AGAIN. LIKE... RIGHT NOW. *TODAY.*

YES.

FUCK YES.

It was the early 90s. Cell phones and internet were uncommon, and the department stores still processed their sales with 20+ year-old tech.

The December 26 crowds were thick with gift returners and bargain hunters. Retail *chaos*.

This was going to be a cinch.

We beelined to JCPenney's. Big crowds, tired staff, no receipt needed for refunds.

We "borrowed" a gift box, slipped an ugly sweater into it, and took it to the returns desk.

They gave us 35 bucks.

Dahlkemper's was next. Frankie found a loose gift bag, I dropped in a matching denim jacket and jeans.

45 bucks.

Overpriced Sears gave us a whopping *64 dollars* for *another* pair of college sweatshirts.

And with our "winnings" Frankie bought a black faux-leather jacket off the clearance rack that fit her *perfectly*.

MERRY. FUCKING. CHRISTMAS.

We blew the rest on pizza and comics.

We'd successfully and *spontaneously* pulled off the low-rent suburban equivalent of the Big Score.

I felt like a badass. More importantly, Frankie did too.

But I never did anything like that *ever* again.

MALL ENTRANCE

After the holidays I decided to apply for some loans and ended up moving back to my out-of-state college to finish my degree.

Pretty soon we'd both met other people and broke things off.

It's a *hard* time, living in those cracks between childhood and adulthood. Hard to figure out who you are and how you're going to live your life...

...hard to find a friend to share it all with.

But trying to be "cool" too?

Forcing yourself to be someone you *aren't?*

That's *always* a disaster.

Ryan Dunlavey - May 2017

141

TROLLING FOR LESBOS

Gabby Rivera

I'm fifteen and I think I'm gay and I hate everything.

My mom's in the kitchen cooking *arroz con gandules* and pork chops. *Jeopardy*'s on TV. My father's walking into the living room, kissing my mom on the cheek, and plopping onto our big and comfy couch. He will remain on the couch until dinner is served. But he's worked all day and he's the man. So, yeah.

My little brother's upstairs watching *Yu-Gi-Oh!* And I'm here, in the family computer room,[1] panicking. In our Pentecostal Protestant home there was no room for "I think I'm gay-ish?" Or like whatever you called it when late at night, when all the world was sleeping, I would rub one out thinking of Angelina Jolie and Salma Hayek kissing. (And also being best friends and giggling, naked . . . ?) But in this family computer room, I was trying to research homosexuality while holding my breath, waiting for someone to push open the computer room door and expose me.

The late nineties was a quaint and totally wild moment in time where all of us had to dial up the internet and wait, with bated breath, for it to pick up and link us to the World Wide Web. AOL was the internet, and chatrooms were like running comment sections. All usernames were anonymous. No one had blue checks by their names, and you could

---

[1] Family computer room: Computers couldn't fit in pockets when I was a kid. They needed their own rooms. My family had a tiny office and we shoved the computer in there. My dad's ties hung next to it.

actually sign off when you were done. Like, back when offline was a continuous state of being.

Lycos.com[2] offered me psychological journals on homosexuality and porn. So guess where I found myself? The Women4Women chatroom. Clicking into that room felt like slinking into a gay bar for the first time. I entered, was announced, and then sat quiet for hours just watching the conversation of actual lesbians scroll past my eyes. I had no entry point. I didn't know what I was, I just knew that this chatroom had something to do with my midnight Angelina/Salma self-love sessions.

I was a teenager and nothing fit. Clothes didn't fit 'cause I was thick. Heterosexuality didn't fit. But there I was in that chatroom, anxious as fuck, and also hating everyone in it. The ever-present religious guilt and general anxiety, compounded with all the wild hormones coursing through me, pushed me into this weird space where I wanted to take out all my conflicting and awful feelings on the actual lesbians.

Remember, there was the internet but not any real social media.[3] No Twitter, Tumblr, Instagram. No way to see happy, healthy LGBTQ folks of color thriving and living beautifully in all our queer melanated glory. There was Ellen, Melissa Etheridge, and the Indigo Girls, but the thought of being associated with "manly white lesbians" was terrifying enough to create a whole new level of anxiety for me. Internalized homophobia is a trip. I was already othered by other Puerto Rican kids 'cause I liked to read books and listen to Nirvana; I couldn't handle any more reasons to be cast off into whiteness and cut off from my people.

And then there I was typing Bible verses into the Women4Women chat and reminding people that God created Adam and Eve, not Adam and Steve. And I figured if Mom came in and asked what I was doing, I could just tell her that I was spreading the Gospel.

It became an obsession. Every day, after school, after finishing my homework, and completing all the necessary firstborn-daughter chores, I got to troll the lesbians. My parents thought I was doing extra-credit

[2] Lycos.com was a search engine from a time before there was Wi-Fi and Justin Bieber.
[3] Yo, deadass, no social media!

assignments. Because that's what chubby, bespectacled, curly-haired, brown nerds do: we do homework. Like so much homework that we need extra homework. Meanwhile, I'm telling Lezzie4LittlePlasticCastles[4] that she needs to repent and rebuking the demons out of DykeTYM3.

It got to the point where I'd enter the chat and like half the room would disappear. They'd send me IMs and start fighting back and it freaked me out so I'd block them. Or they'd fold into a private group chat and there'd be no one to harass. Well, except for the men pretending to be lesbians. They'd have screen names like SexyLadyscissor6969696 and were literally one a/s/l[5] from asking to cyber. And ugh talking to those guys was the worst. But still I persisted, 'cause I still wasn't ready to deal with liking other girls and being a good Christian and praying on my knees post-pleasing myself and crying my guts out, pleading with God to wipe the sin from me.

In the middle of one of my shame-the-lesbians sessions, someone messaged me: **Do you want to talk?**

Yo, I totally wanted to talk. Like so bad that when I got that message, I shut down the computer and went right to bed. No self-love. But also, no self-hate.

The next day, I signed on to that Women4Women chatroom and I just sat in my corner and watched. I read what folks were talking about without bringing up Adam and Steve. That same person messaged that same thing: **Do you want to talk?**

I didn't reply. I sat there and read that sentence like a million times. I got up and snuck a bowl of Captain Crunch[6] into the computer room and read it again.

I'm 15 and I think I'm gay and I hate everything.

We messaged until my parents sent me to bed and then late into the night after I snuck out of bed once I heard my parents snoring and signed back online. She was only a few years older than me and was living on the West Coast. She told me about how she came out and what her first girlfriends were like. She also listened. For hours. I told her about my

---

[4] Was literally like, "But how many lesbian jokes can I put into a screen name?" And the answer is I did not put enough.
[5] The AOL Instant Messenger version of "wyd? wya?"
[6] *Con* Crunch Berries.

Angelina/Salma thing and how I had the most ginormous crush on my substitute biology teacher but not on any of my friends.

And soon, we traded chats for late-night phone calls, and then I wasn't crying anymore while I prayed. I'd hang up with her and lie in my bed, feeling like maybe God was okay with all of this. God gave me this body and all the feelings in it, even the freaky sexy ones, and maybe it was all going to be just fine and I wouldn't be damned and I'd be okay. Just like she was.

I was an internet troll. A closeted, brown baby dyke but still a troll. But I gotta say that in some way it's vastly different from trolling now[7] while still also sharing deep-seated roots in internalized homophobia and misogyny. But also, when someone reached for me in an attempt to find my humanity, all of me cracked wide open and I let them. I apologized for my shit. I owned my shit, me, that fifteen-year-old kid. I did that.

We disrupted that narrative, the one that tells you that you shouldn't be a queer and the one that tells you that it's okay to treat women like shit, and we created our own. And now! Now, she's married and has a family with babies in it! And me, well, I'm out here writing *America*, America Chavez's solo series, and just trying to hold space for all the little brown baby queers to feel good in their spirits and bodies. And look at us!

We all fit in the family computer room.

I'm thirty-four and I know I'm queer and I pretty much love everybody.[8]

---

[7] Literally men threatening to rape/kill/violate women because we exist and create and are breathing.
[8] Unless you suppress queer women of color by upholding the white supremacist patriarchy, then icfwu.

THE NEW GODS OF THE AIRWAVES

by Jen Vaughn

THERE ARE MANY OF US WHO ATTEND MORE LIVE PODCAST PERFORMANCES THAN MOVIES OR CONCERTS.

CRIMIN LIVE

THE STORIES AND VOICES KEEP US COMPANY

FROM LONG NIGHTS AT THE DRAWING TABLE...

TO LONG COMMUTES

OCCASIONALLY, WE MUST PAY TRIBUTE—

BAD TIMES ARE TOUGH BUT NOT TOUGHER THAN ME

HEY BOO-BOOS!

STAY SEXY, AND DON'T GET MURDERED

MUSICIANS TAKE APART THEIR SONGS

ALL HAIL THE GLOW CLOUD

JOIN US AS THE SLEEPLESS HOURS TICK PAST

DD NEXT EPISODE

TELL ME ABOUT YOUR TRANS HEADCANONS

by Sfé R. Monster

Growing up was lonely. I didn't yet have the language to describe myself that I have today.

queer

non-binary

trans

asexual

The feeling of otherness... of never quite fitting in, and of not knowing how to act, or how to be interacted *with*... was extremely isolating.

Making friends was difficult...

Well what *do* you want?

I don't know!

young sfé

(an ex)

It's not you, it's me.

(inevitably...)

Dating was disastrous to the point of becoming impossible.

By some fluke, while fumbling around in the library card catalog when I was 14, I found a VHS copy of "Boys Don't Cry." Watching it, finally, I saw a person that felt like "me."

transgender content: YEAH!

...ultimately raped & killed for being trans: ...not so great.

It was a reflection of myself, absolutely, but a traumatic one.

It was difficult to feel valid—to feel *anything* good or positive or normal about myself, without any positive trans role models (in real life, or in stories). So... in that absence, knowing what I now knew about myself, and with the few words I'd learned, I began to reinterpret the characters I felt a kinship with from the geek media and stories I loved... as trans.

TINTIN — TRANS GUY

LUKE SKYWALKER (STAR WARS) — TRANS + ACE

QUATRE (GUNDAM WING) — TRANS + GAY

FRODO (THE LORD OF THE RINGS) — TRANS + ACE

BACK TO THE FUTURE
MARTY McFLY
TRANS GUY

THE HUNGER GAMES
PEETA MELLARK
TRANS GUY

There was a common thread to all these characters (with admittedly a lot of self-inserted projection of my own). The honest and earnest young protagonist, underestimated, slightly eccentric, a little obnoxious, and romantically unavailable. An "other," even among his peers. To me, just beginning to discover my own queer identity, these characters became trans men, trans masculine, and incredibly affirming and important.

I thought it was a sneaky subversion— something only I'd ever thought to do. Then, one day, meandering around the internet, I discovered the term:

TRANS HEADCANONS

A headcanon is a personal opinion or theory for a fictional character. A trans headcanon simply means choosing to interpret a character as trans— something I was already well versed at doing!

and what if...

omg yeah!

trans (war) boy

demi trans guy

NUX
MAD MAX: FURY ROAD

NEWT
PACIFIC RIM

Talking about trans headcanons online opened up new doors, new discussions... a whole new community to talk and relate to! All sorts of people, who all felt the same way about these characters that I did!

trans girl

non-binary

nobody in this show is cis or straight

MABEL PINES
GRAVITY FALLS

LINK
THE LEGEND OF ZELDA

SUMMER, RICK & MORTY
RICK & MORTY

Suddenly, I wasn't alone, people were seeing the same things I was seeing, and still loved these characters! It was validating, and so incredibly affirming.

Nobody needs a reason or any proof to headcanon a character as trans. They just can be. They just are.

As I continue to transition, and as I reclaim parts of myself that I once rejected and had difficulty accepting, new nonbinary, agender, and genderqueer headcanons have risen up in importance to me.

Not to mention a recent influx of in-canon, contextual, queer, trans, and asexual characters involved as integral parts of the stories, movies, comics, and games that I currently love has given me something new to take comfort, rejoice in, and celebrate.

"Undertale" blew me away with its inclusion of queer, trans, lesbian, bi, gay, and nonbinary characters (including a nonbinary protagonist!)

Trans headcanons have helped me plot my own transition, and given me confidence and courage in my every-day life.

They've given me a way to see myself in stories where I never could before, and confidence and courage in my own appeal and self-worth.

I've learned that if people still love and are attracted to characters they are choosing to interpret as trans... that means someone could love and be attracted to me, too.

And for me, that's the most empowering and validating feeling on the planet.

SCRIPT: *GERARD WAY* ART: *ROBERT WILSON IV* COLORS: *KELLY FITZPATRICK* LETTERS: *RYAN FERRIER*

I'M IN LOVE WITH THE SPACE.

THE SPACE BEHIND THE PLACE INSIDE YOUR HEAD.

HALLELUJAH!

MOMENT OF IMPACT.

NICE TO MEET YOU.

THIS IS SOMETHING I LOVE--

THE INSTANT THAT THE IMAGES AND WORDS YOU ARE SEEING PROCESS IN YOUR "MIND'S EYE".*

"Fribgndgh"

SUPERCOSMIC

AND THIS IS WHAT IT FEELS LIKE TO ME.

SO I'LL TELL YOU WHAT I BELIEVE HAPPENS WHEN YOU READ COMICS YOU LOVE AND SHARE YOUR CREATIVITY WITH THE UNIVERSE.

*THANK YOU, SCOTT MCCLOUD.

THIS IS THE FANCY ZONE. FLIGHTS OF FANCY, YOUR FANCY, I'M FANCY, THE DRAPES ARE FANCY.

THE FANCY ZONE IS WHAT OCCURS OUTSIDE THE BRAIN, SLIGHTLY ABOVE AND A MEASURE BEHIND THE SKULL.

WHEN YOUR MIND IS COMPLETELY BLOWN.

IT IS AN EXPLOSION OF EMOTIONALLY CHARGED INSPIRATION, FEELINGS, AND THOUGHTS--GENERATED, ABSORBED, OR A COMBINATION OF THE TWO.

WHEN THE HAIRS STAND UP ON THE BACK OF YOUR NECK AND THE CROWN OF YOUR HEAD TINGLES--THAT'S THE FANCY ZONE DOING WHAT IT DOES BEST--CONNECTING TO THE MAGINAX.

AND WHAT'S THE MAGINAX?

THE MAGINAX IS A CONNECTION--FROM YOUR PSYCHOSPIRITUAL BRAIN-CORE--

LEADING OFF FROM THE TOP OF THE SKULL--

--THROUGH GALAXIES, AND DIRECTLY INTO THE ALL-COSMIC COMMUNAL EXPANSE INHABITED BY DREAMERS LONG PASSED, WHERE IDEAS AND INSPIRATION--

ALL RIGHT--I BELIEVE ALL OF THAT STUFF, BUT THAT ISN'T WHY I'M EXPLAINING IT TO YOU.

I'VE STRUGGLED WITH TALKING ABOUT LOVE, SO I DECIDED TO TALK TO YOU ABOUT SOMETHING I LOVE DOING.

BUT IT FELT LIKE I WAS AVOIDING THE TOPIC, "LOVE", SO I'VE DECIDED TO BAIL ON THAT. WE CAN TALK ABOUT THE REST SOME OTHER TIME.

...

THIS IS GOING TO GET BORING IF I'M JUST STANDING HERE TALKING TO YOU.

HMMMM... THIS ALLOWS ME TO HIDE BUT WILL ALSO GET BORING...

THE SUBJECT OF LOVE IS DIFFICULT FOR ME. I IMAGINE IT MAY BE DIFFICULT FOR A LOT OF PEOPLE.

IT TOOK ME A LONG TIME TO UNDERSTAND IT. TO GET GOOD AT IT, TO ACCEPT IT, AND TO STOP HATING MYSELF SO MUCH.

BEFORE THAT HAPPENED THERE WERE LONG NIGHTS IN CROWDED CONCRETE BOXES. MOVING, SOUND DRONING, WAITING.

I'M STANDING AGAINST THE WALL AND WATCHING THE PEOPLE BECAUSE I AM SO VERY ALONE. BUT I'M OK WITH IT BECAUSE I'VE LEARNED OVER THE YEARS HOW TO CLIMB INTO MY HEAD TO GET AWAY FROM THAT FEELING.

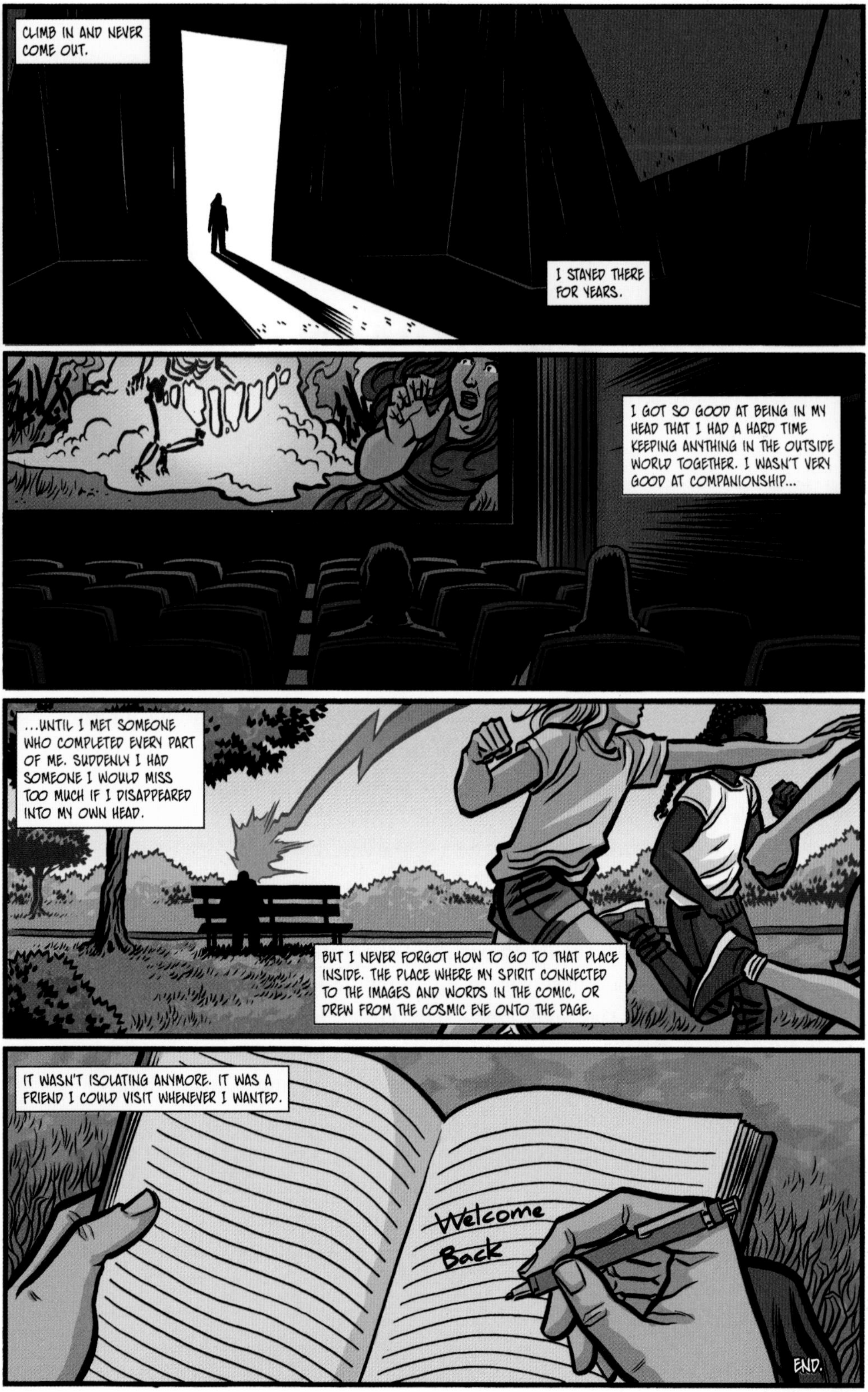
CLIMB IN AND NEVER COME OUT.
I STAYED THERE FOR YEARS.
I GOT SO GOOD AT BEING IN MY HEAD THAT I HAD A HARD TIME KEEPING ANYTHING IN THE OUTSIDE WORLD TOGETHER. I WASN'T VERY GOOD AT COMPANIONSHIP...
...UNTIL I MET SOMEONE WHO COMPLETED EVERY PART OF ME. SUDDENLY I HAD SOMEONE I WOULD MISS TOO MUCH IF I DISAPPEARED INTO MY OWN HEAD.
BUT I NEVER FORGOT HOW TO GO TO THAT PLACE INSIDE. THE PLACE WHERE MY SPIRIT CONNECTED TO THE IMAGES AND WORDS IN THE COMIC, OR DREW FROM THE COSMIC EYE ONTO THE PAGE.
IT WASN'T ISOLATING ANYMORE. IT WAS A FRIEND I COULD VISIT WHENEVER I WANTED.
Welcome
Back
END.

LOVE IN ALDERAAN PLACES

JP Larocque

I hate *Star Wars*. There. I've said it.

To hate America's beloved epic space opera isn't particularly noteworthy, as many people hate all sorts of beloved franchises. In fact, the more beloved the franchise and the more fervent the fan base, the more common it is to find terrifying contrarian trolls roasting it on various internet forums, in the comments section of fan videos, or offering up "hot takes" in those obnoxiously pervasive think pieces you see on Twitter. (Editors at *Slate*: Call me!)

But to hate *Star Wars* AND be a self-avowed gay geek of a certain generation is . . . well, dangerous. It's not really done. It's breaking from the tribe, and can lead to bullying, social exclusion, and, eventually, death.

Well, maybe not the death part. But a legitimate fear of judgment, and one that played a crucial role in my initial lie to John, which set us on a path . . . to the Dark Side. Dun DUN DUHHHHH.

Now who is John? First, let me backtrack a little bit.

You see, in my life, I've come out many times, and as many things.

I came out of my mother's womb as a massive baby, for instance. Twelve pounds, and twenty-six inches long. The hospital staff used to prop me up on the nurses' station desk like some sort of carnival oddity. I'm not sure how this was legal, but things were very different in an era largely characterized by Stephen King telefilms and childhood abduction.

A few years later, I came out of an oxygen tent as a sickly four-year-old, clutching a vomit-stained Barbie named Delores. My grandmother would whisk her away, wash and brush her hair, and supply her with a brand-new dress. "She just needed to change her outfit to look her best," she would say. I would smile, then puke on her, and then the cycle would begin again.

In my late teens, I came out as gay, which shouldn't be that surprising given my previous anecdote about Delores. But it was more of a theoretical gay than a practical gay in terms of actual physical contact with other gay human beings, and was mostly lonely save for the Sears catalogs in my parents' home. God bless those male underwear models.

And then I came out as a gay geek. Now *here* was the real homecoming.

You see, roughly around the same time that I was perving on the male underwear models, I was also obsessively consuming geeky popular culture. We're talking Batman and Superman and the Teenage Mutant Ninja Turtles. There was Ellen Ripley, brandishing her flamethrower and murdering a bunch of aliens in a look that was just androgynous enough for a tiny beige homosexual to replicate on the schoolyard without attracting much attention. And there were those X-Men, a group of morose-but-sexy outcasts with superpowers and totally ripped bodies that were *basically me*, you guys.

Here lies JP Larocque. Morose but sexy, lover of spandex, lasers for eyes.

Being a geek was a comfort to me, and it was definitely tied to my sexual development, but for some reason I didn't think to imagine that there would be other gay geeks like me out there. So I spent a few years futzing about the dating scene and pretending to like lots of stuff that I didn't care much about, like dodgeball and Mariah Carey and dodgeball (why do gays like dodgeball so much?), all the while wondering if any other gay men were as deeply invested in Michelle Pfeiffer's iconic performance as Catwoman in *Batman Returns*. And then I came out, and realized that LOTS of gay men loved Pfeiffer's Catwoman. LOTS.

I found my tribe, and I felt like I belonged somewhere. I could talk about New Caprica on a date (actually happened) or interrupt sex to defend Raimi's use of organic web shooters in *Spider-Man* (actually happened) or unpack the value of *Jessica Jones* on a loud patio at a leather bar (actually happened). And dudes felt safe to approach and discuss their various geeky obsessions, and we'd always find a halfway point.

Until John.

John found me, really. He was a big fan of my web series *Gay Nerds*, and tracked me down via one of those gay dating apps with a name like Crushr or Grater or Smashr or something that sounds like what a serial killer does to a corpse after they're done with it. And unlike most of the men who would message me, his profile photo had a human face rather than just a torso. We started talking, and once I was confident that he was not an actual serial killer, we arranged a date.

He looked exactly like his photo, which was a sexy relief. Square-jawed, broad-shouldered, and perfect for cosplay. There was gateway space talk, with *Battlestar Galactica* and *Babylon 5* and, eventually, *Star Trek*. There was a lot of *Buffy the Vampire Slayer* gushing, and some in-depth analysis of the Marvel Cinematic Universe. He seemed to tolerate my defense of *Alien 3*, and I was willing to look past his affection for *Man of Steel*.

Things were promising, you guys. Like, I wasn't googling rustic barn weddings, but I was imagining what it would be like to introduce him to my friends and family. And he was smart and funny! The banter was 50% Whedon, 30% Sherman-Palladino, 20% Kevin Williamson. The quips were flying fast and super nineties. We went on more dates, and things seemed to be building to something.

Well . . . that something was *The Phantom Menace*. Yup.

There's that moment you dread on a date that creates a dividing line between genuine happiness and qualified happiness. It's never a total deal breaker, mind you, but it's when the rose-colored glasses slide down your nose and you get a chance to see things as they really are, which is . . . disappointing. Human. Tolerable. When things go from lover to life partner. Like you'll accept it so you don't die alone, but you imagine yourself in your fifties washing stained underwear and listening to him snore or bitch about how you're cooking too many sweet potatoes and you start thinking instead about that hot guy you winked at during Fan Expo back in your twenties who was probably your soulmate.

This feels like a therapy conversation.

Anyhow, we were out for dinner, and I made a joke about *The Phantom Menace* being bullshit, and he—wait for it—*defended* it.

Now, everyone knows *The Phantom Menace* is garbage. The only thing anyone even remembers about that film is the CGI pod race, all of the weird racism, and the feeling of a million childhoods being smashed to pieces by George Lucas. I remember leaving the theater with my father on opening night and looking at all the shell-shocked faces. People were stunned at how bad it was. Stunned.

Well, John not only defended it, but he also got irritated by my lack of reverence for the series. Compared to some of our playful, irreverent banter, my comments had hit a nerve, and I wasn't prepared for him to be quite so serious. *Star Wars* was really important to him, and he'd seen all the films multiple times. I tried to backtrack by mocking Hayden Christensen's lines about sand in *Attack of the Clones*, but this actually made it so much worse.

Silence fell over the table. I could tell that I needed to do something to save the evening. Save the whole relationship, really. Prevent myself from dying alone. A life of sweet potatoes and stained underwear, but by myself.

So, I lied.

I said I was so disappointed by the prequels because I loved the original trilogy so much. That *Star Wars* was our generation's Harry Potter, and that it had sexy Harrison Ford in it, and it had kick-ass Carrie Fisher in it, and that it basically invented blockbuster movies. At the very least, it was full of glowing phalluses being brandished around and daddy issues galore and a tiny troll says "Size matters not," all of which should allow it a place in the gay pantheon. It was *important*.

None of this was true because I didn't just hate the prequel trilogy, I hated the original trilogy. I hated the sequel and standalone films. I hated the expanded universe, including all novelizations, cartoons, comic books, action figures, and video games. I thought George Lucas was a hack, and that he could keep his kissing siblings and Lego robots and queens and endless conversations about trade embargoes and Rebel Alliances and metal bikinis and beep beep boop boop boop.

But John was so relieved. That familiar warmth had returned to his face, and he looked at me with—dare I say it? A new hope. That night we made love, and it was beautiful.

Wouldn't it be lovely if it all ended there? That I told one little fib about loving *Star Wars*, and then we would quietly retire into partnered bliss? That we'd get married, adopt hundreds of babies, and live a long and fruitful life together? I mean, lots of couples keep secrets from each other. Secrets between lovers are the lifeblood of Western civilization.

And then, on my deathbed, I'd pull our children close and hiss "I hate *Star Wars*" into their puzzled faces before shuffling off this mortal coil. It would be perfect. Too perfect.

Oh, what a tangled web we weave when first we practice to deceive. Because the lies didn't stop. They couldn't stop. John loved *Star Wars* too much, and now that I loved *Star Wars*, *we* loved *Star Wars*.

- There was an initial DVD rewatch, starting with the prequel series (because he wanted to walk me through what was good about it), followed by the originals (*The Empire Strikes Back* twice because it was that good).
- There was the *Star Wars Holiday Special*, followed by two television films about Ewoks, followed by the cartoons *Star Wars: Droids*, *Star Wars: Ewoks*, *Star Wars: The Clone Wars*, and *Star Wars Rebels*.
- When he'd sleep over, he'd read passages from Timothy Zahn's *Thrawn* trilogy, which he adored.
- A passing reference I made to Carrie Fisher being awesome led to a birthday cake shaped like Princess Leia.
- He would update me daily on set reports from the new sequel trilogy, and would make us watch films starring those actors as some sort of emotional preparation.
- He was dead set on a couple's costume for Halloween. He would be Han Solo, and I would be Leia.
- He got angry at me when I accidentally knocked over his *Millennium Falcon* toy while cleaning and didn't talk to me for two whole weeks.

And I was fine. Totally and utterly fine. Really, I couldn't possibly have been more fine. I was taking up kickboxing, and going to the gym, and every target was a tiny C-3PO.

So what was the straw that broke the proverbial camel's back?

On a regular old Saturday afternoon, I decided to rewatch *Alien 3*. Oh, the cool comfort of Fiorina 161, rainy prison planet and home to bald convicts and child autopsies and a depressed Ripley struggling with her own existence in the face of a very real death sentence. God, what a bleak film. Not perfect by any means, but just totally awesome for staying true to the nihilism of the series and for ending Ripley's story with such a gut punch. I was in the zone, and that zone was totally David Fincher, circa early nineties.

John walked in, took one look at the screen, and muttered, "This movie sucks."

I LOST MY MIND.

When I flash back to that argument, I don't remember much, except that at one point I said *Star Wars* was "fantastical bullshit" and that "none of it made any sense" and that I had tolerated six months' worth of "Natalie Portman speaking in a robot voice" and "flying cars" and "terrifying teddy bears murdering people in a forest" while he couldn't deal with two hours of a bald Sigourney Weaver crying in a factory about a dead little girl.

What I do remember vividly was the hope that had flooded his face after my lie had been replaced by utter disappointment, and I knew this was an argument our relationship probably wouldn't be able to weather. We stayed together for a few more weeks, but it felt over, and when we decided to go our separate ways, he told me I should have just been honest with my feelings about the franchise instead of lying about it. He was right. I mean, I don't know if that honesty would have led to a relationship, but perhaps that would have been for the best?

So, the moral of the story:

Don't "Force" yourself to be someone you're not?

If you lie, you'll end up riding "Solo"?

Don't look for love in "Alderaan" places?

Or perhaps this is just another coming-out process for me as I continue to refine my geeky self. Another peel of the onion, only this one made a *Star Wars* nerd cry. Perhaps I'll find me a man who really likes the *Alien* franchise, and the sexy *X-Men*, but who also hates stupid *Star Wars*.

Stupid, dumb *Star Wars*.

Stupid, dumb, boring *Star Wars*.

I wonder if *Slate* is hiring.

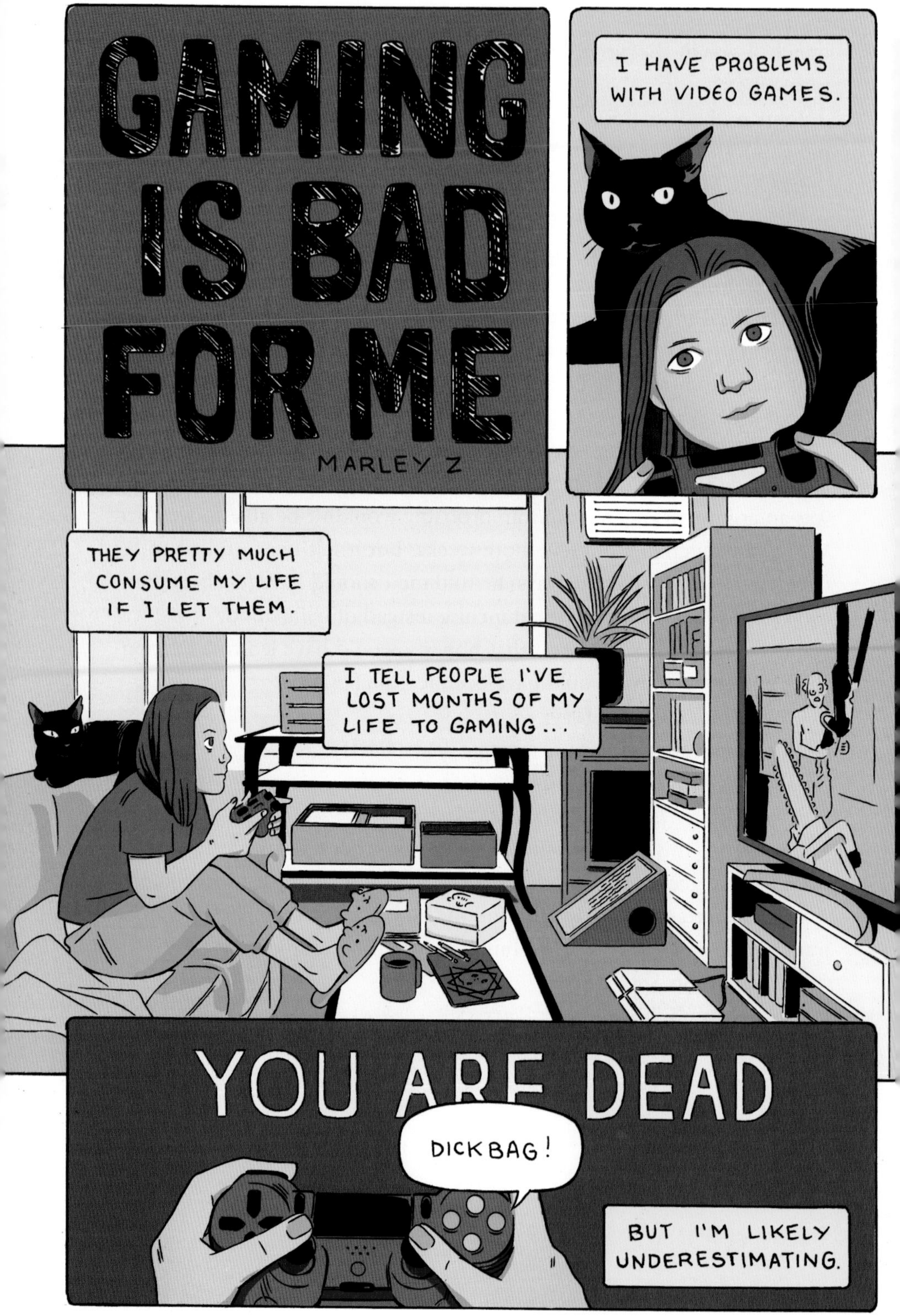
GAMING IS BAD FOR ME
MARLEY Z
I HAVE PROBLEMS WITH VIDEO GAMES.
THEY PRETTY MUCH CONSUME MY LIFE IF I LET THEM.
I TELL PEOPLE I'VE LOST MONTHS OF MY LIFE TO GAMING...
YOU ARE DEAD
DICKBAG!
BUT I'M LIKELY UNDERESTIMATING.

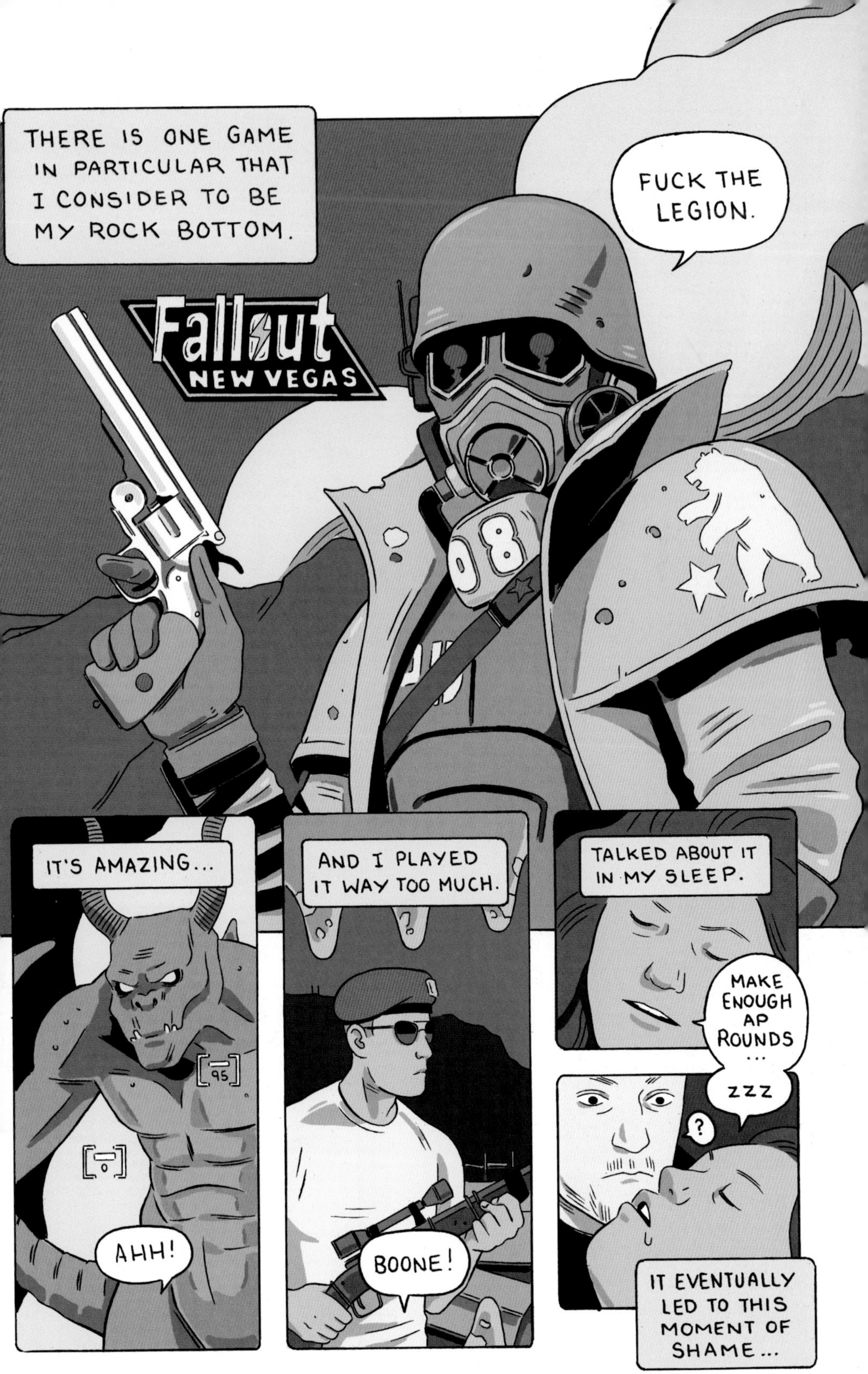
THERE IS ONE GAME IN PARTICULAR THAT I CONSIDER TO BE MY ROCK BOTTOM.
FUCK THE LEGION.
Fallout NEW VEGAS
IT'S AMAZING...
AHH!
AND I PLAYED IT WAY TOO MUCH.
BOONE!
TALKED ABOUT IT IN MY SLEEP.
MAKE ENOUGH AP ROUNDS...
ZZZ
?
IT EVENTUALLY LED TO THIS MOMENT OF SHAME...

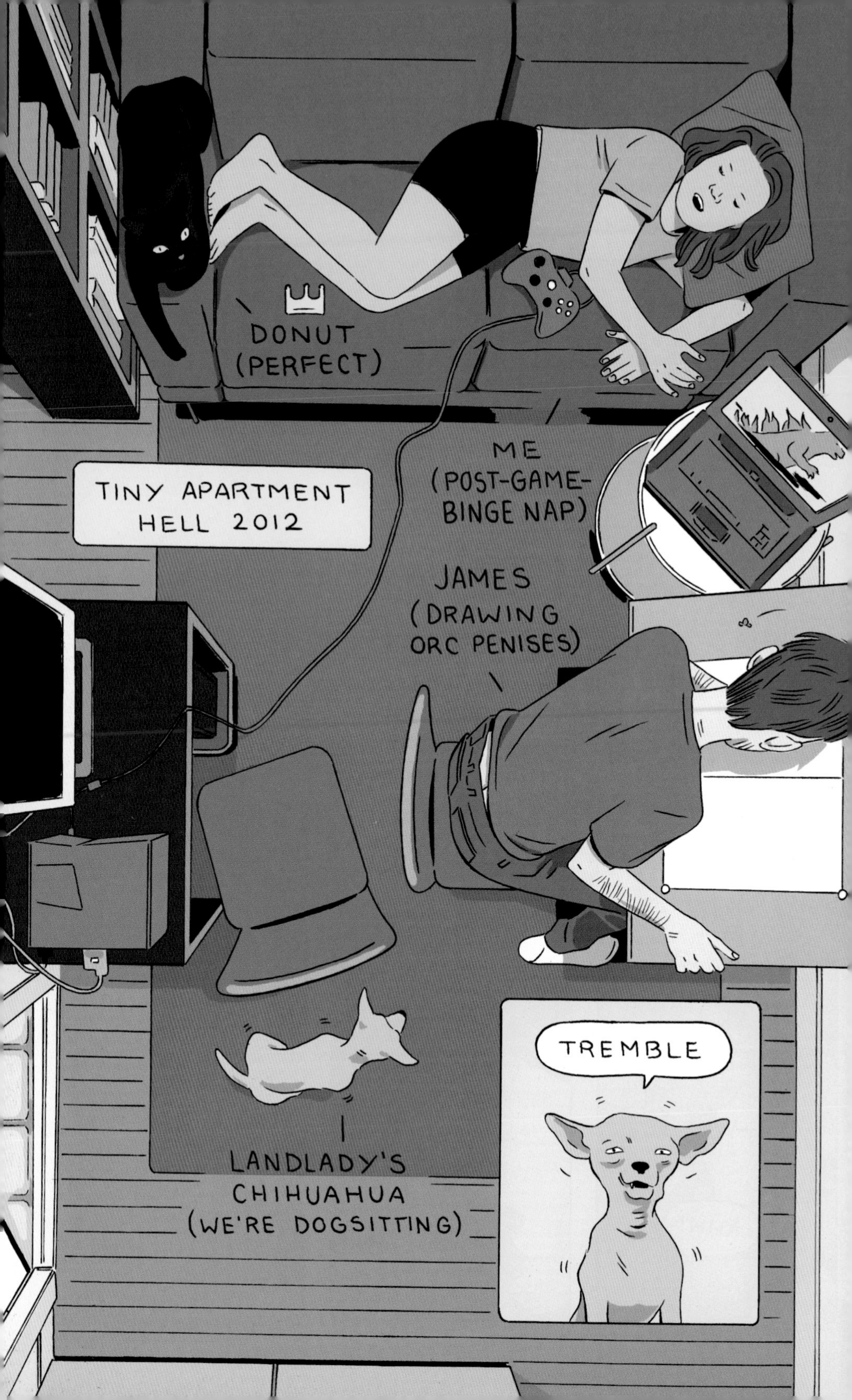
TINY APARTMENT HELL 2012
DONUT (PERFECT)
ME (POST-GAME-BINGE NAP)
JAMES (DRAWING ORC PENISES)
LANDLADY'S CHIHUAHUA (WE'RE DOGSITTING)
TREMBLE

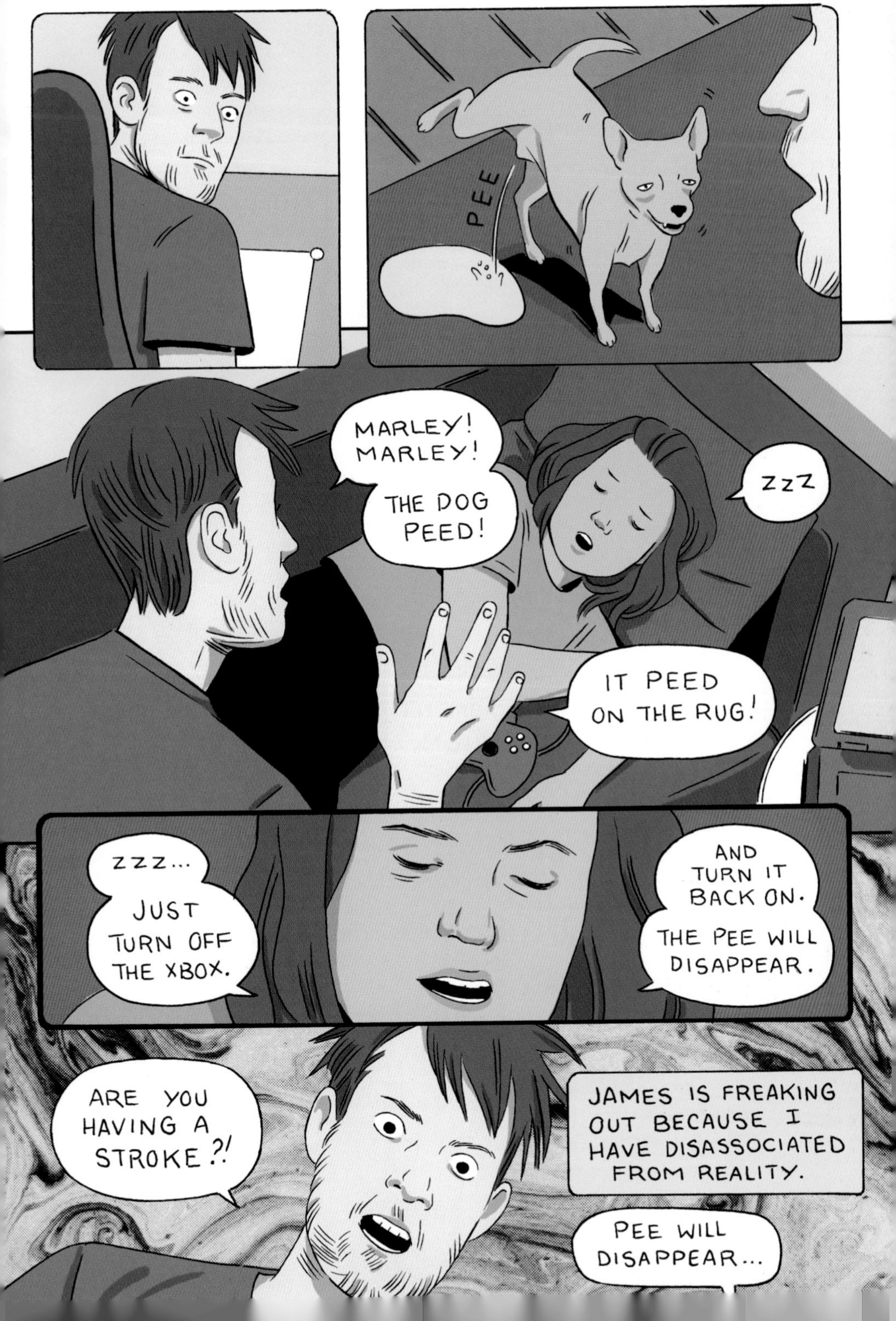
PEE
MARLEY! MARLEY!
THE DOG PEED!
ZZZ
IT PEED ON THE RUG!
ZZZ...
JUST TURN OFF THE XBOX.
AND TURN IT BACK ON.
THE PEE WILL DISAPPEAR.
ARE YOU HAVING A STROKE?!
JAMES IS FREAKING OUT BECAUSE I HAVE DISASSOCIATED FROM REALITY.
PEE WILL DISAPPEAR...

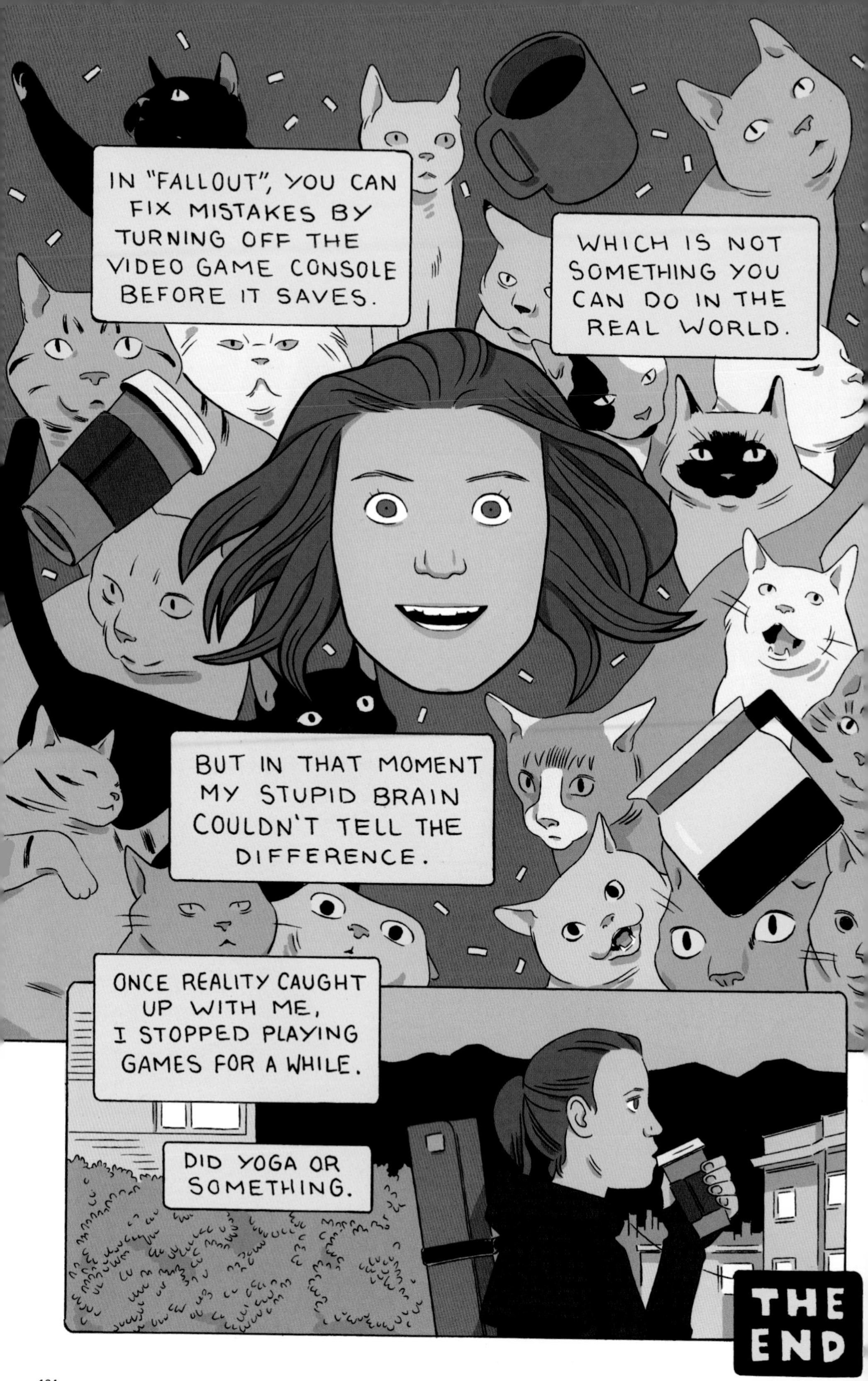
IN "FALLOUT", YOU CAN FIX MISTAKES BY TURNING OFF THE VIDEO GAME CONSOLE BEFORE IT SAVES.
WHICH IS NOT SOMETHING YOU CAN DO IN THE REAL WORLD.
BUT IN THAT MOMENT MY STUPID BRAIN COULDN'T TELL THE DIFFERENCE.
ONCE REALITY CAUGHT UP WITH ME, I STOPPED PLAYING GAMES FOR A WHILE.
DID YOGA OR SOMETHING.
THE END

WHAT GIRLS WANT

Speranza

There was a Tumblr meme that circulated a couple of years ago and that you still see around sometimes. It's the kind they call a snowclone—that is, a repeatable phrase that forms a kind of template when you put in new variables, like "X is the new Y" or "Putting the X into Y" or "One does not simply walk into Y"—almost like a plug-and-play proverb: instantly customizable. This particular meme was based on a line from the Good Charlotte song "Girls and Boys" (2002) and it goes like this: "Girls don't like boys, girls like X and Y."

In the original song, the lyric was "Girls don't like boys, girls like cars and money," which is so depressingly clichéd and sexist, it's hard to believe it. Girls like cars and money, girls are gold diggers willing to put out sexually for rich guys, yawn; heard it. How can a major pop act still put this kind of boring, misogynist claptrap into a song? But there you go, that's mainstream culture for you, still repeating visions of women that haven't the slightest glimmer of personality or originality and can't withstand the slightest scrutiny: girls don't like boys, girls like *cars* and *money*—really? You've *talked* to a lot of girls, have you?

What's wonderful is what geek girl culture did with the meme: even the quickest of searches gets you variations of delightful, specific, recognizable female authenticity:

Girls don't want boys, girls want high-speed internet and dragons.

Girls don't want boys, girls want bisexuality properly represented in media.

Girls don't want boys, girls want fundamental human rights and affordable bras.

Girls don't like boys, girls like birds and Netflix.[1]

Girls don't like boys, girls like the old layout with the same GIF dimensions.

Girls don't like boys, girls like cars and Monet.

Girls don't like boys, girls like accurately depicted female armor in movies.

Girls don't like boys, girls like pretty underwear and emotionally damaged superheroes.

Girls don't like boys, girls like that part in *Rogue One* where the two star destroyers crash together in slow motion.

Girls don't like boys, girls like genetically engineered supersoldiers and crushing the patriarchy.

Like many snowclones, some of these alter the formula a bit—misquoting a little, messing with or otherwise altering the sentence structure (*like* vs. *want*; not always giving both an X and a Y)—but they're all clearly variations on a theme. And what variations! Each line is a poem that can be read closely for meaning. Girls like genetically engineered supersoldiers *and* crushing the patriarchy: is that a statement of girls' infinite variety (*we like comic book heroes and are also feminists*), or a way of rethinking and reclaiming the comic book heroes themselves (*feminists like genetically engineered*

---

[1] This, like so many memes, refers to another something else that went viral on the internet; in this case, the YouTube video of a young girl who replies, defiantly, when asked if she likes boys or girls, "I like Netflix and birds!" https://www.youtube.com/watch?v=kdCMfycBVVY.

supersoldiers, so give us the Captain America we deserve!)? Liking both pretty underwear and emotionally damaged superheroes claims superhero comics for girl culture, intentionally and deliberately feminizing a genre more typically associated with teenaged boys. These memes, unlike the boring lyrics of the Good Charlotte song, aren't replicating the stereotypes of a sexist mass culture: they're challenging and changing them.

Beyond any individual example, we can see general trends in the meme responses. Perhaps unsurprisingly, considering that this is an internet meme, we have girls declaring their allegiance to techno-geek culture (in the form of high-speed internet and usable web design); they are also making feminist statements (desiring affordable bras, crushing the patriarchy) and articulating various other progressive goals (like bisexual representation and fundamental human rights). We have puns (cars and Monet) and other deliberately humorous conjunctions (like the high tech/low tech of internet and dragons), which let the meme writers showcase their wit and personality. And we also have various gestures toward geek culture and fandom: not just classic science fiction and fantasy (*Star Wars*, dragons, accurately depicted female armor) but also comics (emotionally damaged superheroes, genetically engineered supersoldiers) and of course, Netflix, where we can binge watch all our favorite shows, especially those starring Natalie Dormer.

There are so many versions of the meme featuring Natalie Dormer that it's worth pausing a moment to consider them. Check out examples like:

Girls don't like boys, girls like space travel and Natalie Dormer.

Girls don't like boys, girls like Natalie Dormer and jeans with actual pockets.

Girls don't like boys, girls like Natalie Dormer doing the ice bucket challenge.

Girls don't like boys, girls like Natalie Dormer and kittens.

Girls don't want boys to like them, girls want Kristen Stewart and Natalie Dormer to play lesbian lovers in an indie movie with a good soundtrack.

Girls don't like boys, girls like Natalie Dormer and . . . that's it, really. Girls like Natalie Dormer.

They really do! And if you do, you can buy T-shirts, tote bags, and other merchandise with "Girls don't like boys, girls like Natalie Dormer" printed on it at sites like Redbubble. While you occasionally see other famous women name-checked in the meme—fandom favorites like Gillian Anderson (*girls don't like boys, girls like aliens and Dana Scully*), Emma Watson, Kristen Stewart, or Tatiana Maslany, for example—Natalie Dormer seems to be not only the current darling of girls who like girls and WLW more broadly, but also, to use the words of the Daily Dot's Gavia Baker-Whitelaw, the current "queen of geek culture."[2] Why?

Baker-Whitelaw's article takes a fair stab at answering the question, citing Dormer's roles in fan-favorite movies and television shows like *Game of Thrones*, *The Tudors*, *The Hunger Games*, *Captain America: The First Avenger*, *Neverwhere*, and of course, *Elementary*. Baker-Whitelaw also points out that Dormer has "carved out a niche for herself as a character actress rather than a romantic lead or ingénue," and also that she is refreshingly straightforward and articulate in interviews; another way of saying this might be to say that Dormer has somehow managed a career in which she has been able to maintain and perform brains, subjectivity, and personhood. Unlike the barely sketched-out girl who likes cars and money, Dormer's roles require specificity: she performs not just intelligence, but high-level machinations. As Anne Boleyn in *The Tudors* and as Margaery in *Game of Thrones*, she performs characters who are playing games of high-stakes chess for their very lives. As Cressida in *The Hunger Games*, Dormer plays a rebellious film director: the woman controlling the camera rather than the object in front of it. Lastly, in *Elementary*, Dormer is absolutely convincing as both "The Woman," Irene Adler, and as Holmes's most brilliant nemesis, Moriarty: Natalie Dormer doesn't like boys, she likes Sherlock Holmes and controlling the entire world as a criminal overlord. So it's fair to say that geek girls like Natalie Dormer for the same reason that they like the *girls don't like boys* meme itself: because it's a way to get away from clichéd, paint-by-numbers representations of women.

---

[2] Gavia Baker-Whitelaw, "How Natalie Dormer Became the Queen of Geek Culture," https://www.dailydot.com/parsec/natalie-dormer-fan-guide/.

It's also a statement of queer desire, of course—and with the first clause being *girls don't like boys*, we should not be surprised that the meme has often emphasized that indeed, *some girls also like girls*, sexually speaking. That said, it would be wrong to see the meme as only, or solely, about sex. The *girls don't like boys, girls like X and Y* meme has many other echoes in women's history and writing; we might think of the famous passage in Virginia Woolf's essay *A Room of One's Own*, which states unequivocally that "Chloe liked Olivia." While Chloe's liking of Olivia has certainly been taken up as that rare textual assertion of desire between women, it's worth considering the line in context. Virginia Woolf is reading a book by a woman writer when she turns the page and . . .

I turned the page and read . . . I am sorry to break off so abruptly. Are there no men present? Do you promise me that behind that red curtain over there the figure of Sir Charles Biron is not concealed? We are all women you assure me? Then I may tell you that the very next words I read were these —"Chloe liked Olivia . . ." Do not start. Do not blush. Let us admit in the privacy of our own society that these things sometimes happen. Sometimes women do like women.[3]

This quotation obviously opens to a queer reading, especially considering Woolf's playful and coy tone here. Her insistence that we should neither start nor blush seems to imply that this must be one hell of a secret—maybe even, you know, *that* sort of secret. *These things sometimes happen*, despite Queen Victoria's supposed (and likely apocryphal) unwillingness to believe in lesbian sex. Woolf's teasing, mock shocked tone seems to suggest that she is winking or waggling her eyebrows at women who love women: *Chloe doesn't like boys, Chloe likes Olivia*, so to speak.

But that's not the only way to read the line, or the meme. Woolf takes pains to emphasize that "Chloe liked Olivia" is a groundbreaking sentence when it comes to women's representation in fiction because this is the first time she can remember seeing two women depicted as friends. In fact, they're more than friends, they're *coworkers*: as Woolf reads on, we discover that:

"Chloe liked Olivia. They shared a laboratory together. . . ." I read on and discovered that these two young women were engaged in mincing liver, which

[3] Virginia Woolf, *A Room of One's Own* (Albatross Publishers, 2015; reprint of 1929), p. 85.

is, it seems, a cure for pernicious anaemia; although one of them was mar-
ried and had—I think I am right in stating—two small children.[4]

In other words, romantic relationship aside, these two women *work* together; they are *scientists*, medical researchers sharing a lab. This sort of thing is catnip to geek girls and female fans, and if it sounds famil-iar—well, it's an earlier version of what has come to be known as the Bechdel Test. The Bechdel Test, as formulated in Alison Bechdel's comic *Dykes to Watch Out For*, asks whether a work of fiction features at least two women or girls who talk to each other about something other than a man. Bechdel was of course influenced by Woolf, among others, but it's worth noting that the strip shows two women sighing and walk-ing past fictitious science-fiction and fantasy movies that *don't* pass the test (*The Barbarian! The Vigilante!*). Published in 1985 (in the midst of a massive geek-culture craze that started after *Star Wars* and lasted well into the 1980s), the strip tells us that the last movie that passed "the test" for women was *Alien* (1979), which starred Sigourney Weaver as Ripley and Veronica Cartwright as Lambert. So we can conclude that, then as now:

Girls don't like boys, girls like Sigourney Weaver as Ripley.

The Bechdel Test can be used to gauge the possibility of a lesbian rela-tionship in a story: after all, two women are needed for a ship, textual or slashy, and many cult films and geek shows don't even have two female characters in their whole cast, let alone on screen at the same time or talking. But the Bechdel Test can also tell us whether a story features well-drawn female characters *full stop*. This, ultimately, is the larger point of *A Room of One's Own*—that women in fiction have historically been seen only from the male writer's limited perspective, and so have been written with no interiority, purpose, or complication. Virginia Woolf is making a case for women writers in this essay. She is outraged that women are limited to the role of love interest and never get pursuits, agendas, and friends of their own. "Suppose," Woolf declares, "that men were only represented in literature as the lovers of women, and were never the friends of men, soldiers, thinkers, dreamers; how few parts in the plays of

---

[4] Ibid., p. 86.

Shakespeare could be allotted to them; how literature would suffer!" So it's not just that Chloe likes Olivia—though she most certainly does!—it's that a woman writer has imagined Chloe as a well-rounded character with interests beyond romance and women friends that she shares those interests with. Or, to meme-ify it:

Girls don't like boys, girls like stories with great female characters.

Girls don't like boys, girls like stories about female scientists.

Girls don't like boys, girls like reading stories written by women writers.

Girls don't like boys, girls like to work, think, dream, and play with other girls.

It's worth noting that this last point—*girls don't like boys, girls like to work, think, dream, and play with other girls*—is true even when (or maybe especially when) whatever they're doing seems to be *about* boys. Janice Radway realized this was true of women who read romance novels: you might think that romance readers are man obsessed, but mainly women who read romance novels like to talk to other women who read romance novels (and not to men! In fact, they're reading romance novels instead of talking to men). Barbara Ehrenreich, Elizabeth Hess, and Gloria Jacobs came to a similar conclusion in their 1985 essay on Beatlemania, a phenomenon that would seem to be about boys if ever there was one. But was it? In fact, Ehrenreich, Hess, and Jacobs describe Beatles fandom just as many of us would describe media fandom today: as a game girls organize and play among themselves—that is, with other girls. They quote one woman describing a scene that any fangirl of today would recognize:

I especially liked talking about the Beatles with other girls. Someone would say, "What do you think Paul had for breakfast?" "Do you think he sleeps with a different girl every night?" Or "Is John really the leader?" "Is George really more sensitive?" And like that for hours.[5]

---

[5] Barbara Ehrenreich, Elizabeth Hess, and Gloria Jacobs, "Beatlemania: Girls Just Want to Have Fun," in *The Adoring Audience*, ed. Lisa A. Lewis (London: Routledge, 1992), p. 87.

Girls knew that they were never going to marry the Beatles; in fact, Ehrenreich, Hess, and Jacobs suggest that for many girls, a lack of access to the real boys wasn't a bug but a feature. Still others felt that their obsession with the Beatles was more about identification than desire: "I wanted to be like them," one woman said, "something larger than life." Another female interviewee claimed, "Now that I've thought about it, I think I identified with them, rather than as an object of them. I mean, I liked their independence and sexuality and wanted those things for myself . . ."[6]

Girls don't like boys, girls like talking about boys with other girls.

Girls don't like boys, girls want independence and sexuality for themselves!

We can see both of these things in today's fandom too: for instance, fan fiction writers and readers, whether they enjoy gen, het, slash, femmeslash, or anything else, are often in a position where they don't just *want* but also *want to be like* the characters they're writing and reading about, regardless of gender. Constance Penley famously framed this as whether you wanted to *be* or *have* a particular character:[7] do female fans want to *be* or *have* Han Solo, *be* or *have* Sherlock Holmes, Mr. Spock, Hermione Granger, Harry Styles, Emma Swan, Steve Rogers? The answer is almost always *both*: girls want both *to be* and *to have* these characters, even when—or maybe especially when—it seems to be all about the boys. This holds true both in hetfic where fangirls are wild for Edward Cullen or the Doctor or in slash fandom where the girls love Dean and Castiel both, Will and Hannibal both. Traditionally, fandom's favorite BSOs—beloved sex objects—were male characters who female fans, gay, straight, poly, ace, or queer, wanted both to *have* and also to *be*. Today, as parts for women get meatier and female fans are becoming more open about their sexuality, we see more and more women filling these roles and playing BSOs that female fans of all sexual stripes both desire and admire. And to confuse the matter even more, remember that even when girls read stories about male characters,

---

[6] Ibid., p. 103.
[7] Constance Penley, "Feminism, Psychoanalysis, and the Study of Popular Culture," in *Cultural Studies*, ed. Lawrence Grossberg, Cary Nelson, and Paul Treichler (New York: Routledge, 1992), p. 488.

they are reading male characters *as they are written by other girls*, because female fans who read fanfic are reading, overwhelmingly, the work of women writers. Virginia Woolf would be so proud.

> Girls don't like boys, girls like reading about boys the way girls write them.

In conclusion, one of the best things about geek girl culture and fandom culture today is that we've all become *very, very good* at specifying what we like—with likes, kudos, hearts, bookmarks, and tags—oh, lordy, the tags. A glance at the Archive Of Our Own's word cloud of popular tags will give you a pretty good idea of some of the things that fangirls like. We like:

alternate universes, angst, BDSM, blood, consent, crack, crossovers and fandom fusions, cuddling & snuggling, drama, education, family, feels, female characters, fights, fingerfucking, firsts, flashbacks, fluff, food, friendship, frottage, future, gore, happy endings, hurt/comfort, intoxication, jealousy, kinks, kissing, language, LGBTQ themes, loss, love, marriage, mental heath issues, misunderstandings, modern era, mythical beings, nonconsensual, orgasms, pain, panic, pining, poetry, polyamory, porn, pregnancy, protectiveness, romance, science fiction & fantasy, secrets, slash, slavery, slow builds, smut, soulmates, suicide, supernatural elements, teams, teasing, tension, threesomes, time travel, topping, torture, tragedy, trauma, travel, violence, voyeurism

It was of course Sigmund Freud who most famously framed the question: *What do women want?* It's still asked, mostly disingenuously: that is, by men of men in such a way that implies not only that they don't want to hear the answer (which they don't) but that no answer could possibly exist anyway (because "woman" in this context is more or less a mythological character). The question of what women want is rarely asked of real women (of whom I know many) but of "woman," that fictional creature of story and song. But in my experience, I find that if you ask an actual, real woman what she wants, she'll happily tell you. And the parts of the internet that geek girls have built or have taken over are full of interesting answers to this question; these are places where geek girls, young and old, are cheerfully, easily, casually describing what they want.

I STARTED READING *HARRY POTTER* AS A FRESHMAN IN COLLEGE.

A FRIEND RECOMMENDED IT AS A FUN BREAK BETWEEN MY HEAVIER READINGS.

AND IN READING, I DISCOVERED...

I HAD A LOT IN COMMON WITH A FICTIONAL, PREPUBESCENT BOY.

I WAS ALSO AN ORPHAN. I HAD ALSO LIVED IN A HOME WHERE PEOPLE RESENTED AND MISTREATED ME FOR IT.

I ALSO ONLY STARTED FEELING ALIVE WHEN I WENT AWAY TO SCHOOL...

...WHERE I ALSO COULD FINALLY ADMIT THE BIG SECRET I HAD HIDDEN FROM PEOPLE WHO WEREN'T LIKE ME.

FOR HARRY IT WAS BEING BORN MAGIC IN A MUGGLE WORLD. FOR ME, IT WAS BEING BORN GAY IN THE DEEP SOUTH...

...SADLY, WITHOUT ANY MAGIC.

SO MAYBE IT SHOULDN'T HAVE SURPRISED ME WHEN HARRY BECAME A PART OF MY COMING-OUT STORY...

...BUT IT DID.

Harry Potter *and the* Awkward Coming-Out Story

Writer
Amanda Deibert

Artist
Cat Staggs

Letterer
Ryan Ferrier

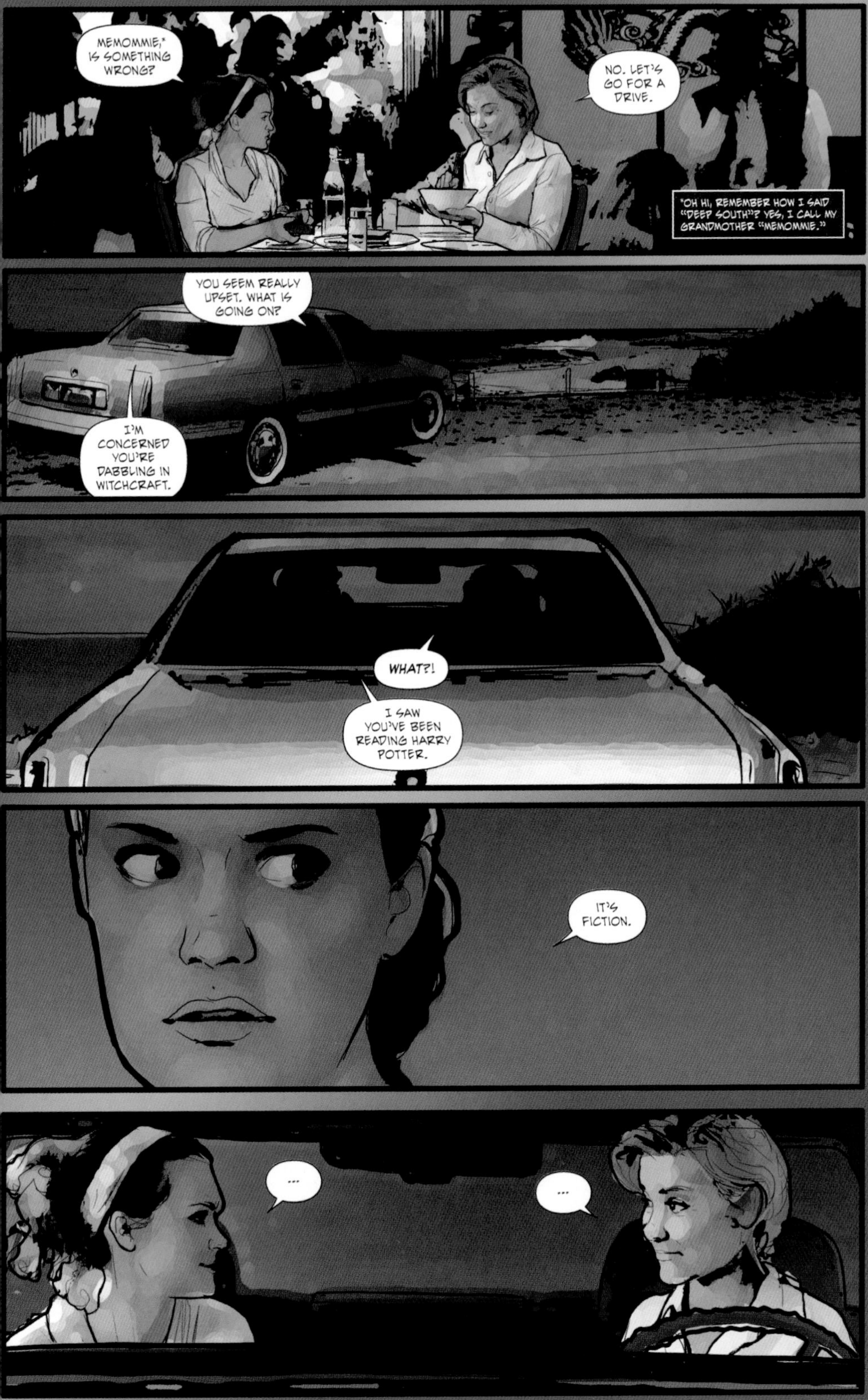
MEMOMMIE,* IS SOMETHING WRONG?
NO. LET'S GO FOR A DRIVE.
*OH HI, REMEMBER HOW I SAID "DEEP SOUTH"? YES, I CALL MY GRANDMOTHER "MEMOMMIE."
YOU SEEM REALLY UPSET. WHAT IS GOING ON?
I'M CONCERNED YOU'RE DABBLING IN WITCHCRAFT.
WHAT?!
I SAW YOU'VE BEEN READING HARRY POTTER.
IT'S FICTION.
...
...

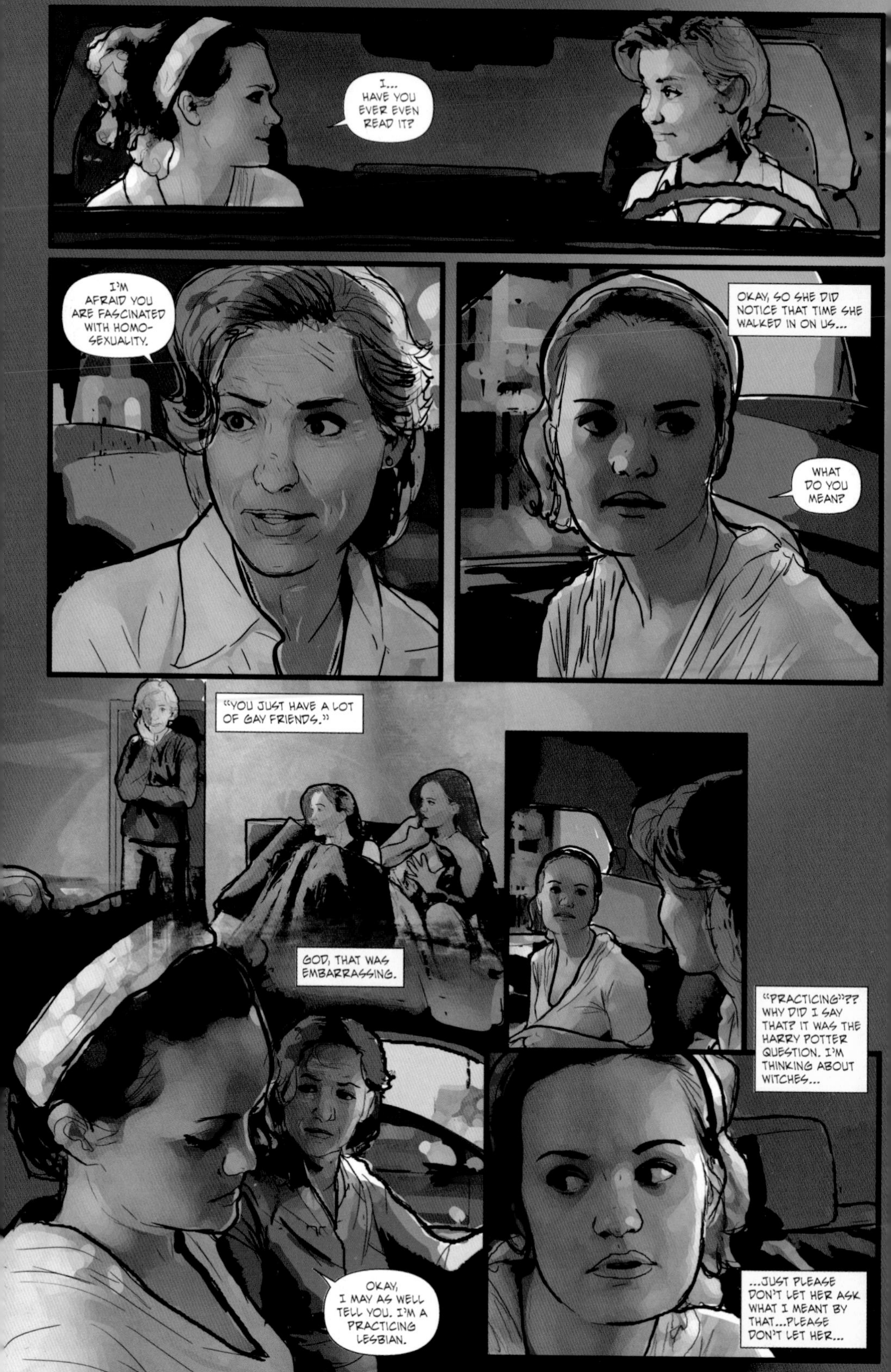
I... HAVE YOU EVER EVEN READ IT?
I'M AFRAID YOU ARE FASCINATED WITH HOMO-SEXUALITY.
OKAY, SO SHE DID NOTICE THAT TIME SHE WALKED IN ON US...
WHAT DO YOU MEAN?
"YOU JUST HAVE A LOT OF GAY FRIENDS."
GOD, THAT WAS EMBARRASSING.
OKAY, I MAY AS WELL TELL YOU. I'M A PRACTICING LESBIAN.
"PRACTICING"?? WHY DID I SAY THAT? IT WAS THE HARRY POTTER QUESTION. I'M THINKING ABOUT WITCHES...
...JUST PLEASE DON'T LET HER ASK WHAT I MEANT BY THAT...PLEASE DON'T LET HER...

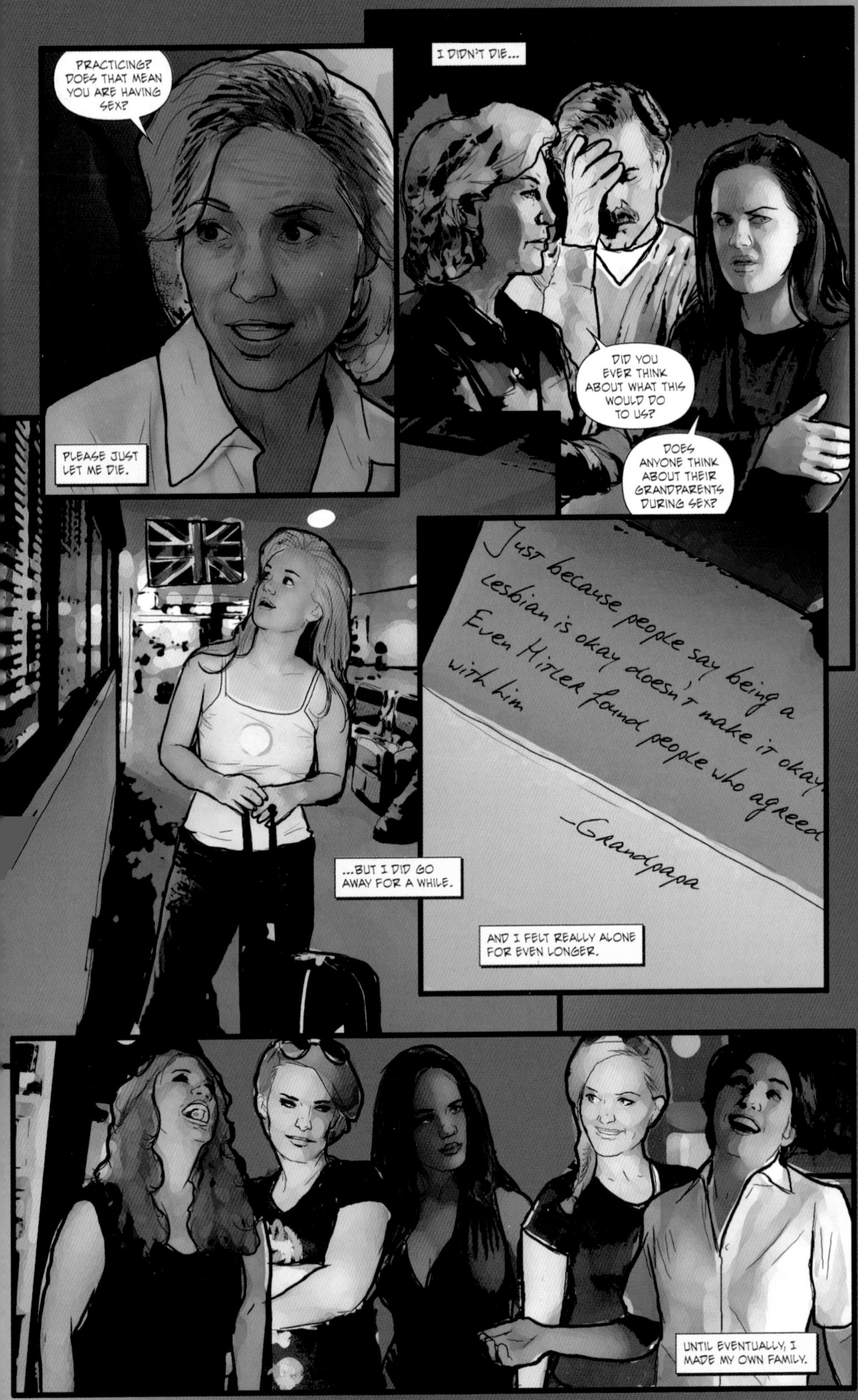
PRACTICING? DOES THAT MEAN YOU ARE HAVING SEX?
PLEASE JUST LET ME DIE.
I DIDN'T DIE...
DID YOU EVER THINK ABOUT WHAT THIS WOULD DO TO US?
DOES ANYONE THINK ABOUT THEIR GRANDPARENTS DURING SEX?
...BUT I DID GO AWAY FOR A WHILE.
Just because people say being a lesbian is okay doesn't make it okay. Even Hitler found people who agreed with him
-Grandpapa
AND I FELT REALLY ALONE FOR EVEN LONGER.
UNTIL EVENTUALLY, I MADE MY OWN FAMILY.

AND FOUND MY OWN LOVE.*

*WHO ALSO HAPPENS TO BE THE TALENTED ILLUSTRATOR DRAWING THESE PAGES.

THAT FAMILY GREW.

AND NOW I GET TO SHARE MY LIFE AND MY LOVE (INCLUDING MY LOVE OF HARRY POTTER) WITH MY OWN LITTLE GIRL.

AND SHE'LL GROW UP IN A NON-MUGGLE FAMILY WHO LOVES HER NO MATTER WHO OR WHAT SHE GROWS UP TO BE.

SO, MAYBE I AM A LITTLE BIT MAGIC AFTER ALL.

End

Dear 1st Love

by Vita Ayala
& Jessi Jordan

It's taken me a long time since we last saw each other, but I finally figured out what Love is.

Love is defending her when the popular girls smile to her face but talk bad behind her back.

Love is doing hours of extra research for a project because the teacher paired us together, and I want her to get the best grade possible.

Love is writing a story for her where she is the hero--the prettiest, the smartest, the bravest-- who gets the boy in the end, just to see her smile.

Love is sitting silently next to each other for hours, trading comics back and forth.

Love is watching an entire series in Japanese with no subtitles, even though I don't speak Japanese.

Love is going to her graduation and being proud, even though I won't be graduating this year.

179

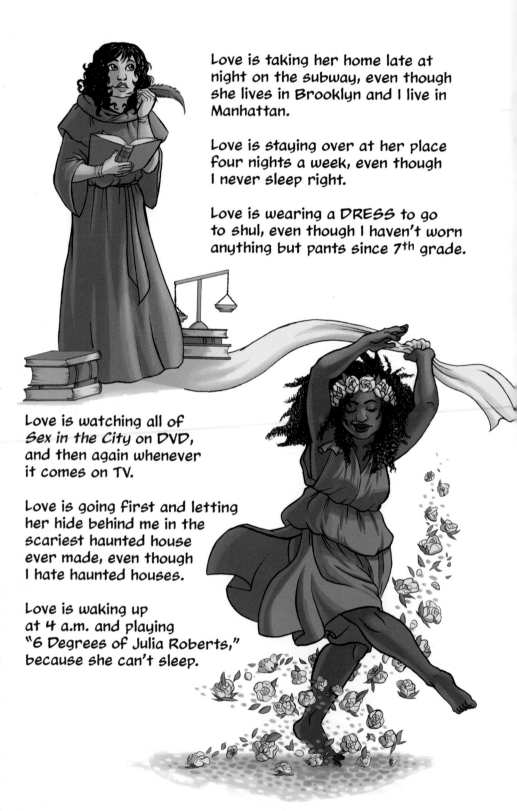

Love is taking her home late at night on the subway, even though she lives in Brooklyn and I live in Manhattan.

Love is staying over at her place four nights a week, even though I never sleep right.

Love is wearing a DRESS to go to shul, even though I haven't worn anything but pants since 7th grade.

Love is watching all of *Sex in the City* on DVD, and then again whenever it comes on TV.

Love is going first and letting her hide behind me in the scariest haunted house ever made, even though I hate haunted houses.

Love is waking up at 4 a.m. and playing "6 Degrees of Julia Roberts," because she can't sleep.

Love is having philosophical arguments until 2 a.m. on Halloween.

Love is listening to old vinyls instead of writing that 15-page paper.

Love is not dating him, because he deserves to be with someone who can be happy with a man.

Love is spending two weeks of the summer being a light tech on a musical she is (assistant) stage managing.

Love is typing up her papers as she dictates them to me, even though I have four of my own to get done.

Love is watching her four nieces and nephews over multiple weekends when asked last minute, because I love them too.

Love is going all the way
out to Brooklyn just for breakfast,
even though I live in the Bronx.

Love is actually enjoying
sharing the shower.

Love is looking forward
to text messages.

Love is making her smoothie before
mine, because I want to be sure I
use the best fruit for hers.

Love is the soft, warm feeling
I get when she is grumpy.

Love is wanting to come
home to her every day,
because there is nowhere
else I'd rather be.

Dear First Love,

I never would have known any of this if
you hadn't taught me that:

Love is sharing your favorite snacks,
even if that means you get less for yourself.

Love is letting you use the last nub of
my favorite crayon because you need
the color for your picture.

Love is playing pretend for hours without
even thinking about turning on the TV.

Love is taking turns being the princess
and the knight, and using kindness to
convince the dragon to be on your side.

Love is forgetting to feel awkward and
stupid and ugly because you think I am
smart and fun and pretty.

Love is that feeling
I get in my chest
when you look at me,
like sitting in the front
seat of my uncle's car
as we speed down a hill.

When I think of Love,
I think of you, my first.

Yours always,

V

THE MULTIFARIOUS MONOLITH OF LOVE

Patrick Rothfuss

A couple days ago, my baby boy smiled at me. A little crooked smile, a smirk.

A few days before that, I got my first smile. Today I got several. He also said "goo" a couple times. I'm not even kidding. It's amazingly cute.

Here's the thing. He also smiled at the ceiling fan. He *really* likes the ceiling fan. Given the choice between the ceiling fan and me, the fan will win three times out of four.

But you know what's strange? I don't mind. I really don't.

I don't mind that he smiles and coos at his mom more than me. It doesn't make me sad that the ceiling fan takes second place, and that almost any window with sunlight behind it is a close third.

I'm fine being fourth in line for smiles. I'm just happy to be on the list.

Standing there, holding my new baby, I had a strange sort of revelation. I was feeling a type of love that was in no way jealous.

I think this might be the purest type of love.

Here's the thing. I'm not a fan of LOVE as a singular concept. It's a ridiculously broad term that can be applied to pets, sex partners, or Oreos. When a word accretes that many definitions, it becomes virtually nonsensical.

If you're hunting for more specific words for love, Greek is a good language to start with. They have *eros*, *philos*, and *agape*. Those three do a pretty good job of breaking the great multifarious monolith of LOVE into slightly more manageable pieces.

I'm assuming you know about them, but just for reference:

- *Philos* is friend love. Family love.
- *Eros* is "I want to bone you" love.
- Agape is . . . tricky. Some people call it "unconditional love." I've heard it referred to as "True Love," "God Love," or "That love which instills worth."

There's also the lesser-known *storge*: "Kindness love." Which is the sort of love you feel for something that's dependent on you. Like an infant or a dog.

So. I'm standing there, looking at my sweet baby, and he's smiling at the ceiling fan. And I realize I don't mind. I'm just happy that he's happy. I'm just happy that sometimes he smiles at me. I'm just happy he's around.

This is a strange and wonderful sensation. This is, I feel, a different type of love.

Now it might seem like I'm talking about agape-style love here. Or storge. But I'm not. This is something different.

What I'm talking about here is love-without-expectation.

We need to stop for a moment and make a word.

If I'm going to spend some time trying to describe a largely unfamiliar concept, I need a name for it. Love-Without-Expectation-or-Desire just isn't going to work. It's not elegant. A newish concept needs a newish name. It needs its own space to grow. You grok?

Plus I just like making words. It's kind of a thing that I do.

From what I gather the Hebrew concept of "חסד" is pretty close to what I'm looking for here. And it's one of the Sephira, which gives it extra gravitas. Unfortunately, it's not going to work because when you transliterate it, it's spelled *"chesed"* and that looks too much like "cheesed" to me.

Fuck it. I know it's not linguistically sound, but I'm going to call it *elutheria*.

Remember where we were? Me. My baby. Ceiling fan.

I simply love him, and I expect nothing in return. This is strangely, delightfully freeing. I don't feel bad if he pays more attention to his mom. I don't mind that he smiles at the fan, or his big brother.

I don't mind if he falls asleep. I don't mind if he throws up on me.

Elutheria—love which demands nothing. The love that expects nothing.

This is an odd concept for me. Because I am a creature composed almost entirely of expectations.

This isn't entirely a bad thing. The ability to anticipate, desire, and plan is important. It gives us control of our lives. It gives us the ability to see forward in time a little. It gives us the ability to steer our destiny a little so we can avoid wrecking our lives against the rocks.

Not always, of course. Sometimes your ship is going to wreck no matter your best efforts. Shit happens. But if you're able to anticipate the future, you can at least brace for impact. That's better than nothing.

Without the ability to predict and therefore exert control on the future, we are helpless. Subject to the constant random battering of a largely entropic universe.

The ability to predict and anticipate isn't bad. The desire for control isn't bad. If you put those things together with a love for language and a vague compulsion for storytelling, you get *The Name of the Wind*.

If you combine these characteristics with a love of charity and a desire to make the world a better place, you get WorldBuilders.org.

If you combine them with a relationship . . . it's not so good. Because trying to control the people you love isn't good. For one thing, people don't like it. (For the most part.) But also because controlling someone means hanging expectations on them. And if people don't live up to your expectations, you're disappointed. And disappointment leads to frustration and anger. And this spiral continues down to the dark side of the Force.

How much nicer would it be to simply love someone? If you expected nothing from your beloved, you could never be disappointed. Nothing could jeopardize that love. It would be unassailable.

This would be elutheria, the love that expects nothing.

What I'm talking about here, is the diametrical opposite of selfish love.

Selfish love demands things. It demands attention. Most of all, selfish love demands love in return. Typically it usually demands ALL the love in return. It demands primacy. Exclusivity. Ownership. Control.

What I'm talking about here is what's commonly called "romantic love."

Romantic love is championed as being awesome in our culture. It's the sort of love you've seen a thousand times in movies and literature. You've seen it in the lives of your friends and family members. You've probably experienced some version of it yourselves.

It's the sort of love where you see your girl chatting with someone and you feel jealous.

It's the sort of love where you see your guy looking at someone and you feel angry.

It's the sort of love where, narratively speaking, you fall for someone, and they don't love you back, and then you kill yourself. (Actual results may vary.)

It's the sort of love that makes you think it's okay to consider someone "your girl" or "your guy." As if you owned them. As if they were under your control. As if your affection made them somehow beholden to you.

And as I stand there, smiling at my baby (who is smiling at our ceiling fan), I am perfectly happy. And I wonder to myself, "At what point did loving someone become an excuse to be a greedy asshole?"

I bounced my idea off a couple people over the last week or so. Love without expectation. I explained about my baby and the ceiling fan. I talked about the chains of desire . . .

"Well," someone said, "it sounds nice, but I don't think that's something that could exist in an adult relationship."

Several people said this, or something very close to it. These comments came up almost compulsively, in a knee-jerk way.

I think people have this automatic response for two reasons.

First, I think they feel attacked. As if I'm telling them they're loving wrong.

I'm not. That's not what this is about. When I talk about how much I'd like a Tesla, it doesn't mean I think you're a dick for driving a Prius. I'm not trying to start a fight here. I'm looking to discuss an idea.

Second, I think people react badly because, in our culture, elutheria is a profoundly unfamiliar concept. We all grew up reading stories about Lancelot and Guenevere (or permutations thereof).

The Arthurian legend is one of our mythic cornerstones. It echoes through the last thousand years of our art and literature. Well . . . eight hundred years, if we're talking about Lancelot. You see, he wasn't in the original story. The French added him in the 1200s.

And to be fair, it's a better story with Lancelot in it. More drama. More tension. More universal appeal.

The downside? Lancelot and Guenevere are generally held up as the villains of the whole Arthurian shtick. They ruined Camelot. Their dirty, dirty lust wrecked the golden age.

But the truth is, if Arthur hadn't been such a douche about the whole thing, there wouldn't have been any problem. If Arthur had just gotten over himself and admitted that Lance was pretty hunky, it could have been cool. If he'd wanted Gwen to be happy, he should have just stepped aside. Or at least turned a blind eye.

Either that or jumped into the sack with both of them. Because . . . y'know . . . hunky.

Imagine the glorious world we'd be living in if *that* was one of our mythic cornerstones, folks. Imagine a world where slash fiction didn't exist because we were, all of us, constantly living the dream.

Okay, back on track here.

Generally speaking, everyone agrees that Arthur overreacted. But Lance and Gwen? It's their *fault*. They're *traitors*. And we know that traitors deserve the lowest, darkest circle of hell.

And sure, Arthur was a little hot-headed. But it was justified, right? Lance and Gwen, their actions were a betrayal.

What were they betraying?

Expectations.

♥

Those of you who have studied any Buddhism are probably nodding along by this point. Believe me, I'm very aware that the more I roll the concept of elutheria around in my head, the more similar it seems to the four noble truths that lead to the eightfold path.

For those of you who haven't studied Buddhism, here it is in a nutshell:

1. There is suffering.
2. Suffering comes from thwarted desire.
3. Therefore, if you eliminate desire, you eliminate suffering.
4. Profit. Moksha.

There is an unassailable simplicity here. There's a reason I'm fond of Buddhism.

I wish I had a strong closer for you, but I'm not really making an argument here. I'm not heading for a conclusion. I'm merely working out my thoughts in text. Writing things down helps me understand them better. It helps me knock the rough corners off my new ideas. (It's my attempt at Right Understanding, the first step of the eightfold path.)

But is elutheria something a person can realistically achieve?

With my baby, the answer seems to be yes. But then things become more complicated. You see, I have responsibilities.

My older son is four. And while it would be pleasant to simply love him and let the chips fall where they may, if I were to do that, I would be failing him as a parent. I need to provide guidance and discipline. I need to control his base monkey instincts with the hope that he may eventually rise above them and become a fully-formed human being.

There's that word again: Control. It's my job to control him. It's my job to have expectations.

Still, I think discarding elutheria entirely would be like throwing the baby out with the bathwater. There are certain expectations that are essential. I expect him to be polite. I expect him to be honest. I expect him to be mindful and kind.

Those are the requirements for being a good human being. It's my job to guide and coach him until he gets there.

Any expectations beyond that, I should be wary of. I shouldn't expect him to be all those things *all* the time. I shouldn't expect him to be tidy. Or quiet when I'm trying to work.

I shouldn't expect him to be straight, or a Democrat, or a painter. I shouldn't expect him to love books.

Expectation is a trap, you see. There's nothing to be gained from it. I don't feel *more* joy seeing him read because I hoped for it. I only leave myself open to disappointment if he doesn't.

Similarly, my relationship with Sarah consists of more than simple love. We are engaged in the partnership. We maintain a household and the purpose of that household is to raise children that are physically and emotionally healthy.

Her cooperation in these things is essential. I expect it.

But other things? Should I expect her to never ogle the pretty college boys on the track team who jog around town every spring? No. Foolishness. Should I expect her to organize the kitchen the same way I would? To want the same color paint in the dining room? To have dinner cooked and ready for me when I come home from work? Should I expect her to always love me best, and most, and only?

No. I think not. I think that would be selfish and self-centered.

The more of these expectations I can let go of, the happier I will be.

But it's hard. Oh it's hard. It goes against a lifetime full of training. It goes against my obsessive desire to control. It goes against my meticulous nature. It goes against what so many stories have told me is true . . .

CREATOR BIOS

MARGARET ATWOOD
(WRITER, ANGEL CATBIRD)

Margaret Atwood is the co-author—with illustrator Johnnie Christmas—of the Dark Horse graphic novel series, *Angel Catbird*. She also writes other things, such as the novel, *The Handmaid's Tale*. She sometimes draws pictures.

VITA AYALA
(WRITER, OUR WORK FILLS THE PEWS)

Vita Ayala is a writer out of New York City, who has done work for DC Comics (*Rebirth Wonder Woman Annual #1*, *Suicide Squad Most Wanted: Amanda Waller & El Diablo*) and Image Comics (*Bitch Planet Triple Feature #4*), as well as creator-owned work (*Our Work Fills The Pews*, Black Mask Studios). They are also currently moonlighting protecting art at one of NYC's oldest and largest museums.

GWEN BENAWAY
(POET, CEREMONIES FOR THE DEAD)

Gwen Benaway is a trans girl poet of Anishinaabe and Métis descent who has published two collections of poetry, *Ceremonies for the Dead* and *Passage*, and will be publishing her third collection, *Holy Wild*, with BookThug in 2018.

TERRY BLAS
(CARTOONIST, MORBID OBESITY)

Terry Blas is the illustrator/writer behind the comics *Ghetto Swirl* and *You Say Latino*. His work has appeared in the comics *Regular Show*, *Rick and Morty*, and *Adventure Time*, and he also illustrated the drag superhero book, *Mama Tits Saves the World*. His latest book is a fat camp murder mystery titled *Morbid Obesity* to be published by Oni Press.

KRISTIAN BRUUN
(ACTOR, ORPHAN BLACK)

Kristian Bruun is an actor, writer, and producer from Toronto, Canada. He is best known for playing Donnie Hendrix on BBC America's *Orphan Black* and Constable "Slugger" Jackson on CBC's *Murdoch Mysteries*. Kristian lives in Los Angeles and really wants a dog.

CECIL CASTELLUCCI
(WRITER, SOUPY LEAVES HOME)

Cecil Castellucci is the author of books and graphic novels for young adults. Her current books are *Soupy Leaves Home, Shade: the Changing Girl*, and *Don't Cosplay with My Heart*. She is the Children's Correspondence Coordinator for The Rumpus, a two time Macdowell Fellow, and the founding YA Editor at the *LA Review of Books*.

MADDISON CHAFFER
(CARTOONIST, STAY)

Maddison Chaffer is a part-time illustrator and full-time vagabond. She is currently working alongside New Form Digital, Eater Magazine, and independent authors as a book illustrator and comic artist, although she aspires to someday just be really, really old.

AMY CHU
(WRITER, RED SONJA)

Amy Chu left a life of corporate intrigue to become a comic book writer for Marvel, DC, and other publishers. She has scripted stories for many well-known characters including *Red Sonja, Poison Ivy, Wonder Woman, Deadpool* and *Ant-Man*. You can learn more about her on her website **iwritecomics.com**.

CHRISTINA "PEACHES" CORTES
(CARTOONIST, PEACH FUZZ)

Peaches is a transfeminine Latina artist from Voorhees, New Jersey. Since she couldn't become an Imperial stormtrooper, she decided to write comics in the hopes to help create a safe and funny space for her fellow members of the queer community. She currently writes her hit Tumblr comic *Peach Fuzz* from Boston, Massachusetts.

VALENTINE DE LANDRO
(ARTIST, BITCH PLANET)

Valentine De Landro is a Canadian comic book artist, illustrator, and designer. His credits include titles from Marvel, DC Comics, IDW, Valiant, and Dark Horse. He's known for *Marvel Knights: 4* and *X-Factor*. He is the co-creator of *BITCH PLANET* with Kelly Sue DeConnick.

AMANDA DEIBERT
(WRITER, WONDER WOMAN '77)

Amanda Deibert writes television and comic books. Her most recent comic book work includes a story in the *New York Times* #1 bestseller *Love is Love* benefitting the victims of the Pulse Night club shooting in Orlando. She has also written for Sensation Comics featuring *Wonder Woman* and *Wonder Woman '77* for DC Comics, and for *John Carpenter's Tales for a Halloween Night* Volumes 2, 3, and 4.

RYAN DUNLAVEY
(ARTIST, ACTION PRESIDENTS)

Ryan Dunlavey is the artist of the non-fiction graphic novels *Action Presidents*, *Action Philosophers*, and *The Comic Book History of Comics* (all co-created with writer Fred Van Lente), as well as *Dirt Candy: A Cookbook* (written by chef Amanda Cohen). His other comics credits include *Li'l Classix*, *MODOK: Reign Delay*, and *G.I. Joe*.

DYLAN EDWARDS
(CARTOONIST, VALLEY OF THE SILK SKY)

Dylan Edwards is the creator of *Transposes*, *Politically InQueerect*, and *Valley of the Silk Sky*. His work has also appeared in the award-winning anthologies *QU33R*, *No Straight Lines*, and *Beyond Anthology*. In 2016, the National LGBTQ Journalists Association honored him with their Award for Outstanding Transgender Coverage.

CARA ELLISON
(VIDEO GAME DESIGNER)

Cara Ellison is a Scottish author and videogame designer, though she started out making radio at BBC Radio 4 and fell into the land of videogames by accident. She's critiqued most aspects of games in word form anywhere you'd expect to find them, from *PC Gamer* to *The Guardian* and back again. A comfortable solo world adventurer, she wrote a book called *Embed With Games* about travelling the world asking questions about why people make games, and what they are for. Permanently uncomfortable in one type of writing or design, she makes TV shows, comics, videogames, and essays, and, frankly, has difficulty sitting still.

RYAN FERRIER
(WRITER, D4VE)

Ryan Ferrier is a Canadian comics writer and letterer best known for his acclaimed *D4VE* series, *Kennel Block Blues*, *Hot Damn*, and various properties including *Teenage Mutant Ninja Turtles*, *Power Rangers*, and *Sons of Anarchy*.

KELLY FITZPATRICK
(COLORIST, SHADE: THE CHANGING GIRL)

Kelly Fitzpatrick is a comic book colorist who has worked on titles such as *Archie, Josie and the Pussycats*, *BITCH PLANET*, *Gotham City Garage*, *DC: Bombshells*, *Neverboy*, and *Shade the Changing Girl* amongst many others. You can follow her work at **kellyfcolors.com**

SHAUNA J. GRANT
(CARTOONIST, PRINCESS LOVE PON)

Shauna J. Grant, the creator of *Princess Love Pon*, is an artist with the magic power to create cuteness. Born and raised in New York City, she adores all things related to magical girls and *shoujo* and is on a mission to create more diverse art that embodies her passion.

MADDI GONZALEZ
(ARTIST, UNCANNY VALLEY HIGH)

Maddi Gonzalez is the series artist for Space Goat Productions' new comic *Uncanny Valley High*, written by Ian Flynn. She is also a member of the Minneapolis-based artist collective Plus Dog and a character designer/contributing artist for the tabletop game Breakfast Cult.

LEVI HASTINGS
(ARTIST, DECLARATION)

Levi Hastings is an illustrator and cartoonist in Seattle. He is the cover artist for the Lambda Award-winning *Beyond Anthology* and creates editorial and autobiography comics for a variety of publications. Together with writer Josh Trujillo, he is currently at work on the American Revolution queer romance comic, *Declaration*. Find more of his work at **www.levihastings. com** and follow along via Instagram and Twitter **@LeviHastingsArt**.

TINI HOWARD
(WRITER, ASSASSINISTAS *)*
Tini Howard is a writer—of comics, mostly. She lives in the North Carolina wilds in a swamp witch house with her husband and a black cat. **@tinihoward**

PRIYA HUQ
(CARTOONIST, MANA *)*
Priya Huq is a comic artist and illustrator whose work can be seen in anthologies and publications such as *Dirty Diamonds* and The Nib. She makes a comic called *Mana*, which you can read for free at **mindheartmemory.net**.

JESSI JORDAN
(CARTOONIST, SWIM *)*
Jessi is a professional illustrator, comic artist, and writer in Houston, Texas. Her work includes *They Have Issues, Swim, The Adventures of Marni & Edward*, and *Musings*. She also won a coloring contest when she was nine.

MEGAN KEARNEY
(CARTOONIST, BEAUTY AND THE BEAST *WEBCOMIC)*
Megan Kearney lives in Toronto where she manages Comic Book Embassy, a co-work studio dedicated to nurturing indie talent. She is an award-winning webcomic creator and regular contributor to numerous anthologies. Currently Megan writes for *Disney Princess*. **@spookymeggie, thequiety.com**.

MAIA KOBABE
(CARTOONIST, GENDERQUEER *)*
Maia Kobabe is the author and illustrator of *The Thief's Tale*, a medieval fantasy webcomic, and *Tom o'Bedlam*, an Ignatz-nominated single issue that was accepted into the Society of Illustrator's Comic and Cartoon Art annual. Maia's other comics, including the *Genderqueer* series, can be found on Tumblr and Instagram **@redgoldsparks**.

JP LAROCQUE
(WEBSERIES CREATOR, GAY NERDS *)*
JP Larocque is writer, director and producer of the award-winning digital series *Gay Nerds* (gaynerds.tv), as well as the short films *Neutered* (2015) and *Where We Were* (2017). When he's not toiling away on scripts or doing standup, he is a development producer in reality television and can be seen on the MTV/Logo series *1 Girl 5 Gays*.

HOPE LARSON
(WRITER, BATGIRL)

Hope Larson is the Eisner-winning cartoonist behind *A Wrinkle in Time: The Graphic Novel*, and the writer of middle-grade adventure comics *Compass South* and *Knife's Edge*, among others. She co-created *Goldie Vance* for Boom!, and she's currently writing *Batgirl* for DC Comics.

H-P LEHKONEN
(WRITER, IMMORTAL NERD)

H-P Lehkonen is the author of the *Immortal Nerd* webcomic on LINE Webtoon, a humorous queer sci-fi adventure. They also work on several comics anthology projects, and teach networking and webcomics in comic schools in their home country, Finland.

MARINAOMI
(CARTOONIST, TURNING JAPANESE)

MariNaomi is the award-winning author and illustrator of four graphic memoirs (*Kiss & Tell: A Romantic Resume, Dragon's Breath and Other True Stories, Turning Japanese*, and *I Thought YOU Hated ME*) and the upcoming graphic novel *Losing the Girl* (Spring 2018). Her work has appeared in over sixty print publications and has been featured on numerous websites, such as The Rumpus, LA Review of Books, Midnight Breakfast, and BuzzFeed. She is the creator and curator of the Cartoonists of Color Database and the Queer Cartoonists Database. **marinaomi.com**

DIANA McCALLUM
(WRITER, TEXTS FROM SUPERHEROES)

Diana McCallum is the co-creator of the From Superheroes Network, a website specializing in superhero comedy. She writes the web comic *Texts From Superheroes* and hosts the *Talk From Superheroes* podcast.

JAMIE McKELVIE
(CO-CREATOR, THE WICKED + THE DIVINE)

Jamie McKelvie is an artist best known for his creator-owned work *The Wicked + The Divine*. He's also done work for Marvel Comics and art for bands such as CHVRCHES and Tegan and Sara.

SFÉ R. MONSTER
(CARTOONIST, BEYOND: THE QUEER SCI-FI & FANTASY COMIC ANTHOLOGY)

Sfé R. Monster is a trans, queer comics creator, and editor of the Lambda Award-winning *Beyond: The Queer Sci-Fi & Fantasy Comic Anthology*. Sfé lives in Halifax, Canada, is co-founder of Beyond Press, and has a heart that can never be moved far from the sea.

SAADIA MUZAFFAR
(TECH ENTREPRENEUR)

Saadia Muzaffar is a tech entrepreneur and founder of Future of Leadership Lab, which inspires reimagining what it will take to solve big problems and build our collective future.

HOPE NICHOLSON
(WRITER, THE SPECTACULAR SISTERHOOD OF SUPERWOMEN)

Hope Nicholson is the Winnipeg-based owner of the publishing company Bedside Press. She's also written a history of female characters in comics called *The Spectacular Sisterhood of Superwomen* (oh, and she curated and edited this book and its prequel).

HARRIS O'MALLEY
(WRITER, PAGING DR. NERDLOVE)

Harris O'Malley is a writer and dating coach. He runs the geek dating advice blog *Paging Dr. NerdLove* where he dispenses the best relationship advice on the web.

SHEE PHON
(CARTOONIST, I KNOW IT'S NOT ABOUT ME BUT I DON'T WANT TO DIE)

Shee Phon is the creator of *Oneshots*, which includes a variety of short comics ranging from fantasy to autobiography. The most recent, *I know it's not about me but I don't want to die*, debuted at TCAF 2017. She'll be returning to Sheridan College where she hopes to learn new skills to support her in making comics and picture books.

GABBY RIVERA
(WRITER, AMERICA CHAVEZ)

Gabby Rivera is a queer Latinx writer living in Brooklyn, NY. She is currently writing the sold-out, smash hit solo *America Chavez* series for Marvel. Her critically acclaimed debut novel *Juliet Takes a Breath* was called the "dopest LGBTQA YA book ever" by *Latina*. Put simply by Roxane Gay, it's "F***ing outstanding." Gabby's been featured nationally on *SyWire*, *PBS News Hour*, and publications such as *The New York Times*, *Vibe Magazine*, *Refinery29*, and *The Advocate*. Gabby works as the Youth Programs Manager at a national LGBTQ non-profit education network. She's represented by New Leaf Literary & Media, Inc.

CHRIS ROBERSON
(WRITER, iZOMBIE)

Chris Roberson is the co-creator of *iZOMBIE* (with Mike Allred) and *Edison Rex* (with Dennis Culver), and the co-writer of *Hellboy and the B.P.R.D* and other titles set in the world of Mike Mignola's *Hellboy*.

PATRICK ROTHFUSS
(WRITER, THE NAME OF THE WIND)

Patrick Rothfuss is the *New York Times* Bestselling author of *The Name of the Wind*, *The Wise Man's Fear*, and *The Slow Regard of Silent Things*. When not writing, Pat plays with his children, makes mead, and runs **Worldbuilders**, a non-profit that mobilizes the geek community to raise money for charities like Heifer International, Mercy Corps, and First Book.

IVAN SALAZAR
(PR, COMIXOLOGY)

Ivan Salazar works in PR and marketing for the digital comics service comiXology and is based out of Los Angeles, CA. His story in the *The Secret Loves of Geeks* is his first published work but he hopes it's not his last.

DANA CLAIRE SIMPSON
(CARTOONIST, PHOEBE AND HER UNICORN)

Dana Claire Simpson, a native of Gig Harbor, Washington, first caught the eyes of devoted comics readers with the internet strip *Ozy and Millie*. After winning the 2009 Comic Strip Superstar contest, she developed the strip *Phoebe and Her Unicorn* (originally known as *Heavenly Nostrils*), which is now syndicated in over 200 newspapers worldwide. There are five book collections: *Phoebe and*

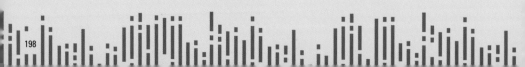

Her Unicorn, Unicorn on a Roll, Unicorn vs. Goblins, Razzle Dazzle Unicorn, and *Unicorn Crossing,* and a graphic novel, *The Magic Storm.*

Simpson's books have appeared on the *New York Times* bestseller list, and won the Washington State Book Award and the Pacific Northwest Book Award. She lives with her husband and her cat in Santa Barbara, California.

SPERANZA
(FANFICTION WRITER)

Speranza is a fan writer, vidder, community mod, and archivist. Her *Stargate: Atlantis* story "Written by the Victors" was one of the ten "classics" selected for Vulture.com's "Fanfiction Syllabus," and her MCU story "4 Minute Window" was recently recced on the Empire Film Podcast. Read an interview with her at **thesecurioustimes.com**.

CAT STAGGS
(ARTIST, CROSSWIND)

Cat Staggs is an artist best known for her work on the *New York Times* bestselling title *Smallville Season 11* from DC Comics. Staggs is currently working on *Crosswind,* written by Gail Simone (Image Comics). She has also worked on popular titles like *Adventures of Supergirl* (DC Comics), *Wonder Woman '77* (DC Comics), *X-Files* and *Orphan Black* (IDW), *Sensation Comics featuring Wonder Woman* (DC), *The Vampire Diaries* (DC), *Phantom Lady and Doll Man* (DC), *Star Trek* (IDW), and over ten years in the *Star Wars* universe with Lucasfilm.

JEN VAUGHN
(CARTOONIST, THE SECRET LOVES OF GEEK GIRLS)

Jen Vaughn is a cartoonist and game designer working under the green trees of Seattle, Washington. Check out her comics *Avery Fatbottom: Renaissance Fair Detective, Deadwater,* and more at **HauntedVaultStudios.com**

MICHAEL WALSH
(ARTIST, STAR WARS)

Michael Walsh is a Canadian comic creator based out of Hamilton, Ontario best known for his work at Marvel Comics on books such as *The Avengers, X-Men,* and *Star Wars.* He has worked for numerous other publishers, illustrating stories featuring *Hellboy, The X-Files,* and *Teenage Mutant Ninja Turtles.* He has also created his own properties, *Comeback* and *ZERO,* with Image Comics.

GERARD WAY
(WRITER, THE UMBRELLA ACADEMY)

Gerard Way is the best-selling co-creator of Dark Horse's *The Umbrella Academy* comic series with Gabriel Bá, and curator of DC's Young Animal imprint.

KATIE WEST
(WRITER, THE SECRET LOVES OF GEEK GIRLS)

Katie West is the owner of Fiction & Feeling publishing company, a photographer, a writer, and the executive assistant to the creators of *The Wicked + The Divine*.

LETTY WILSON
(ARTIST, COSMIC)

Letty Wilson is the artist of award-winning sci-fi series *Cosmic*, written by Erin Keepers. She has contributed to various anthologies and has several other books published with Panels, a collaborative group based in Glasgow, Scotland, including the SICBA award-winning graphic novel *A Stranger Came To Town*.

ROBERT WILSON IV
(ARTIST, HEARTHROB)

Robert Wilson IV is a comic artist and illustrator who currently lives in Dallas, TX. He is the co-creator of *Hearthrob* (with writer Chris Sebela and colorist Nick Filardi) and the artist of *Bitch Planet* issue #3. He is also active in the poster community making tour and concert posters for bands such as The Mountain Goats, Death From Above 1979, and The Sword, among others.

MARLEY ZARCONE
(ARTIST, SHADE: THE CHANGING GIRL)

Marley Zarcone is an American comic artist based out of Kelowna, British Columbia. She is currently on pencils and inks for *Shade: The Changing Girl*, and has worked on such titles as *Effigy*, *Madame Xanadu*, *Teenage Mutant Ninja Turtles*, and *Forgetless*.